FREE Study Skills DVD Offer

Dear Customer,

Thank you for your purchase from Mometrix! We consider it an honor and privilege that you have purchased our product and want to ensure your satisfaction.

As a way of showing our appreciation and to help us better serve you, we have developed a Study Skills DVD that we would like to give you for <u>FREE</u>. **This DVD covers our "best practices" for studying for your exam, from using our study materials to preparing for the day of the test.**

All that we ask is that you email us your feedback that would describe your experience so far with our product. Good, bad or indifferent, we want to know what you think!

To get your **FREE Study Skills DVD**, email <u>freedvd@mometrix.com</u> with "FREE STUDY SKILLS DVD" in the subject line and the following information in the body of the email:

    a.   The name of the product you purchased.

    b.   Your product rating on a scale of 1-5, with 5 being the highest rating.

    c.   Your feedback. It can be long, short, or anything in-between, just your impressions and experience so far with our product. Good feedback might include how our study material met your needs and will highlight features of the product that you found helpful.

    d.   Your full name and shipping address where you would like us to send your free DVD.

If you have any questions or concerns, please don't hesitate to contact me directly.

Thanks again!

Sincerely,

Jay Willis
Vice President
<u>jay.willis@mometrix.com</u>
1-800-673-8175

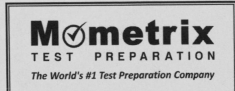

TerraNova
SUCCESS STRATEGIES
Grade 6

TerraNova Test Review
for the
TerraNova, Third Edition

Dear Future Exam Success Story:

First of all, **THANK YOU** for purchasing Mometrix study materials!

Second, congratulations! You are one of the few determined test-takers who are committed to doing whatever it takes to excel on your exam. **You have come to the right place.** We developed these study materials with one goal in mind: to deliver you the information you need in a format that's concise and easy to use.

In addition to optimizing your guide for the content of the test, we've outlined our recommended steps for breaking down the preparation process into small, attainable goals so you can make sure you stay on track.

We've also analyzed the entire test-taking process, identifying the most common pitfalls and showing how you can overcome them and be ready for any curveball the test throws you.

Standardized testing is one of the biggest obstacles on your road to success, which only increases the importance of doing well in the high-pressure, high-stakes environment of test day. Your results on this test could have a significant impact on your future, and this guide provides the information and practical advice to help you achieve your full potential on test day.

Your success is our success

We would love to hear from you! If you would like to share the story of your exam success or if you have any questions or comments in regard to our products, please contact us at **800-673-8175** or **support@mometrix.com**.

Thanks again for your business and we wish you continued success!

Sincerely,
The Mometrix Test Preparation Team

Need more help? Check out our flashcards at: http://MometrixFlashcards.com/terranova

TABLE OF CONTENTS

INTRODUCTION 1

SUCCESS STRATEGY #1 – PLAN BIG, STUDY SMALL 2
INFORMATION ORGANIZATION 2
TIME MANAGEMENT 2
STUDY ENVIRONMENT 2

SUCCESS STRATEGY #2 – MAKE YOUR STUDYING COUNT 3
RETENTION 3
MODALITY 3

SUCCESS STRATEGY #3 – PRACTICE THE RIGHT WAY 4
PRACTICE TEST STRATEGY 5

SUCCESS STRATEGY #4 – PACE YOURSELF 6

TEST-TAKING STRATEGIES 7
QUESTION STRATEGIES 7
ANSWER CHOICE STRATEGIES 8
GENERAL STRATEGIES 9
FINAL NOTES 10

MATHEMATICS 12

PRACTICE TEST #1 67
ANSWERS AND EXPLANATIONS 82
PRACTICE TEST #2 88
ANSWERS AND EXPLANATIONS 103

SCIENCE 109
PRACTICE TEST 114

READING 129
LITERATURE 129
INFORMATIONAL TEXTS 135
PRACTICE TEST 141

ENGLISH 155
PRACTICE TEST 160

WRITING 174
PERSUASIVE TEXT 176
INFORMATIONAL OR EXPLANATORY TEXT 178
NARRATIVES 180
PRACTICE TEST 183

THANK YOU 185

ADDITIONAL BONUS MATERIAL 186

Introduction

Thank you for purchasing this resource! You have made the choice to prepare yourself for a test that could have a huge impact on your future, and this guide is designed to help you be fully ready for test day. Obviously, it's important to have a solid understanding of the test material, but you also need to be prepared for the unique environment and stressors of the test, so that you can perform to the best of your abilities.

For this purpose, the first section that appears in this guide is the **Success Strategies**. We've devoted countless hours to meticulously researching what works and what doesn't, and we've boiled down our findings to the five most impactful steps you can take to improve your performance on the test. We start at the beginning with study planning and move through the preparation process, all the way to the testing strategies that will help you get the most out of what you know when you're finally sitting in front of the test.

We recommend that you start preparing for your test as far in advance as possible. However, if you've bought this guide as a last-minute study resource and only have a few days before your test, we recommend that you skip over the first two Success Strategies since they address a long-term study plan.

If you struggle with **test anxiety**, we strongly encourage you to check out our recommendations for how you can overcome it. Test anxiety is a formidable foe, but it can be beaten, and we want to make sure you have the tools you need to defeat it.

Success Strategy #1 – Plan Big, Study Small

There's a lot riding on your performance. If you want to ace this test, you're going to need to keep your skills sharp and the material fresh in your mind. You need a plan that lets you review everything you need to know while still fitting in your schedule. We'll break this strategy down into three categories.

Information Organization

Start with the information you already have: the official test outline. From this, you can make a complete list of all the concepts you need to cover before the test. Organize these concepts into groups that can be studied together, and create a list of any related vocabulary you need to learn so you can brush up on any difficult terms. You'll want to keep this vocabulary list handy once you actually start studying since you may need to add to it along the way.

Time Management

Once you have your set of study concepts, decide how to spread them out over the time you have left before the test. Break your study plan into small, clear goals so you have a manageable task for each day and know exactly what you're doing. Then just focus on one small step at a time. When you manage your time this way, you don't need to spend hours at a time studying. Studying a small block of content for a short period each day helps you retain information better and avoid stressing over how much you have left to do. You can relax knowing that you have a plan to cover everything in time. In order for this strategy to be effective though, you have to start studying early and stick to your schedule. Avoid the exhaustion and futility that comes from last-minute cramming!

Study Environment

The environment you study in has a big impact on your learning. Studying in a coffee shop, while probably more enjoyable, is not likely to be as fruitful as studying in a quiet room. It's important to keep distractions to a minimum. You're only planning to study for a short block of time, so make the most of it. Don't pause to check your phone or get up to find a snack. It's also important to **avoid multitasking**. Research has consistently shown that multitasking will make your studying dramatically less effective. Your study area should also be comfortable and well-lit so you don't have the distraction of straining your eyes or sitting on an uncomfortable chair.

The time of day you study is also important. You want to be rested and alert. Don't wait until just before bedtime. Study when you'll be most likely to comprehend and remember. Even better, if you know what time of day your test will be, set that time aside for study. That way your brain will be used to working on that subject at that specific time and you'll have a better chance of recalling information.

Finally, it can be helpful to team up with others who are studying for the same test. Your actual studying should be done in as isolated an environment as possible, but the work of organizing the information and setting up the study plan can be divided up. In between study sessions, you can discuss with your teammates the concepts that you're all studying and quiz each other on the details. Just be sure that your teammates are as serious about the test as you are. If you find that your study time is being replaced with social time, you might need to find a new team.

Success Strategy #2 – Make Your Studying Count

You're devoting a lot of time and effort to preparing for this test, so you want to be absolutely certain it will pay off. This means doing more than just reading the content and hoping you can remember it on test day. It's important to make every minute of study count. There are two main areas you can focus on to make your studying count:

Retention

It doesn't matter how much time you study if you can't remember the material. You need to make sure you are retaining the concepts. To check your retention of the information you're learning, try recalling it at later times with minimal prompting. Try carrying around flashcards and glance at one or two from time to time or ask a friend who's also studying for the test to quiz you.

To enhance your retention, look for ways to put the information into practice so that you can apply it rather than simply recalling it. If you're using the information in practical ways, it will be much easier to remember. Similarly, it helps to solidify a concept in your mind if you're not only reading it to yourself but also explaining it to someone else. Ask a friend to let you teach them about a concept you're a little shaky on (or speak aloud to an imaginary audience if necessary). As you try to summarize, define, give examples, and answer your friend's questions, you'll understand the concepts better and they will stay with you longer. Finally, step back for a big picture view and ask yourself how each piece of information fits with the whole subject. When you link the different concepts together and see them working together as a whole, it's easier to remember the individual components.

Finally, practice showing your work on any multi-step problems, even if you're just studying. Writing out each step you take to solve a problem will help solidify the process in your mind, and you'll be more likely to remember it during the test.

Modality

Modality simply refers to the means or method by which you study. Choosing a study modality that fits your own individual learning style is crucial. No two people learn best in exactly the same way, so it's important to know your strengths and use them to your advantage.

For example, if you learn best by visualization, focus on visualizing a concept in your mind and draw an image or a diagram. Try color-coding your notes, illustrating them, or creating symbols that will trigger your mind to recall a learned concept. If you learn best by hearing or discussing information, find a study partner who learns the same way or read aloud to yourself. Think about how to put the information in your own words. Imagine that you are giving a lecture on the topic and record yourself so you can listen to it later.

For any learning style, flashcards can be helpful. Organize the information so you can take advantage of spare moments to review. Underline key words or phrases. Use different colors for different categories. Mnemonic devices (such as creating a short list in which every item starts with the same letter) can also help with retention. Find what works best for you and use it to store the information in your mind most effectively and easily.

Success Strategy #3 – Practice the Right Way

Your success on test day depends not only on how many hours you put into preparing, but also on whether you prepared the right way. It's good to check along the way to see if your studying is paying off. One of the most effective ways to do this is by taking practice tests to evaluate your progress. Practice tests are useful because they show exactly where you need to improve. Every time you take a practice test, pay special attention to these three groups of questions:

- The questions you got wrong
- The questions you had to guess on, even if you guessed right
- The questions you found difficult or slow to work through

This will show you exactly what your weak areas are, and where you need to devote more study time. Ask yourself why each of these questions gave you trouble. Was it because you didn't understand the material? Was it because you didn't remember the vocabulary? Do you need more repetitions on this type of question to build speed and confidence? Dig into those questions and figure out how you can strengthen your weak areas as you go back to review the material.

Additionally, many practice tests have a section explaining the answer choices. It can be tempting to read the explanation and think that you now have a good understanding of the concept. However, an explanation likely only covers part of the question's broader context. Even if the explanation makes sense, **go back and investigate** every concept related to the question until you're positive you have a thorough understanding.

As you go along, keep in mind that the practice test is just that: practice. Memorizing these questions and answers will not be very helpful on the actual test because it is unlikely to have any of the same exact questions. If you only know the right answers to the sample questions, you won't be prepared for the real thing. **Study the concepts** until you understand them fully, and then you'll be able to answer any question that shows up on the test.

It's important to wait on the practice tests until you're ready. If you take a test on your first day of study, you may be overwhelmed by the amount of material covered and how much you need to learn. Work up to it gradually.

On test day, you'll need to be prepared for answering questions, managing your time, and using the test-taking strategies you've learned. It's a lot to balance, like a mental marathon that will have a big impact on your future. Like training for a marathon, you'll need to start slowly and work your way up. When test day arrives, you'll be ready.

Start with what you've read in the first two Success Strategies—plan your course and study in the way that works best for you. If you have time, consider using multiple study resources to get different approaches to the same concepts. It can be helpful to see difficult concepts from more than one angle. Then find a good source for practice tests. Many times, the test website will suggest potential study resources or provide sample tests.

Practice Test Strategy

When you're ready to start taking practice tests, follow this strategy:

Untimed and Open-Book Practice

Take the first test with no time constraints and with your notes and study guide handy. Take your time and focus on applying the strategies you've learned.

Timed and Open-Book Practice

Take the second practice test open-book as well, but set a timer and practice pacing yourself to finish in time.

Timed and Closed-Book Practice

Take any other practice tests as if it were test day. Set a timer and put away your study materials. Sit at a table or desk in a quiet room, imagine yourself at the testing center, and answer questions as quickly and accurately as possible.

Keep repeating timed and closed-book tests on a regular basis until you run out of practice tests or it's time for the actual test. Your mind will be ready for the schedule and stress of test day, and you'll be able to focus on recalling the material you've learned.

Success Strategy #4 – Pace Yourself

Once you're fully prepared for the material on the test, your biggest challenge on test day will be managing your time. Just knowing that the clock is ticking can make you panic even if you have plenty of time left. Work on pacing yourself so you can build confidence against the time constraints of the exam. Pacing is a difficult skill to master, especially in a high-pressure environment, so **practice is vital**.

Set time expectations for your pace based on how much time is available. For example, if a section has 60 questions and the time limit is 30 minutes, you know you have to average 30 seconds or less per question in order to answer them all. Although 30 seconds is the hard limit, set 25 seconds per question as your goal, so you reserve extra time to spend on harder questions. When you budget extra time for the harder questions, you no longer have any reason to stress when those questions take longer to answer.

Don't let this time expectation distract you from working through the test at a calm, steady pace, but keep it in mind so you don't spend too much time on any one question. Recognize that taking extra time on one question you don't understand may keep you from answering two that you do understand later in the test. If your time limit for a question is up and you're still not sure of the answer, mark it and move on, and come back to it later if the time and the test format allow. If the testing format doesn't allow you to return to earlier questions, just make an educated guess; then put it out of your mind and move on.

On the easier questions, be careful not to rush. It may seem wise to hurry through them so you have more time for the challenging ones, but it's not worth missing one if you know the concept and just didn't take the time to read the question fully. Work efficiently but make sure you understand the question and have looked at all of the answer choices, since more than one may seem right at first.

Even if you're paying attention to the time, you may find yourself a little behind at some point. You should speed up to get back on track, but do so wisely. Don't panic; just take a few seconds less on each question until you're caught up. Don't guess without thinking, but do look through the answer choices and eliminate any you know are wrong. If you can get down to two choices, it is often worthwhile to guess from those. Once you've chosen an answer, move on and don't dwell on any that you skipped or had to hurry through. If a question was taking too long, chances are it was one of the harder ones, so you weren't as likely to get it right anyway.

On the other hand, if you find yourself getting ahead of schedule, it may be beneficial to slow down a little. The more quickly you work, the more likely you are to make a careless mistake that will affect your score. You've budgeted time for each question, so don't be afraid to spend that time. Practice an efficient but careful pace to get the most out of the time you have.

Test-Taking Strategies

This section contains a list of test-taking strategies that you may find helpful as you work through the test. By taking what you know and applying logical thought, you can maximize your chances of answering any question correctly!

It is very important to realize that every question is different and every person is different: no single strategy will work on every question, and no single strategy will work for every person. That's why we've included all of them here, so you can try them out and determine which ones work best for different types of questions and which ones work best for you.

Question Strategies

Read Carefully

Read the question and answer choices carefully. Don't miss the question because you misread the terms. You have plenty of time to read each question thoroughly and make sure you understand what is being asked. Yet a happy medium must be attained, so don't waste too much time. You must read carefully, but efficiently.

Contextual Clues

Look for contextual clues. If the question includes a word you are not familiar with, look at the immediate context for some indication of what the word might mean. Contextual clues can often give you all the information you need to decipher the meaning of an unfamiliar word. Even if you can't determine the meaning, you may be able to narrow down the possibilities enough to make a solid guess at the answer to the question.

Prefixes

If you're having trouble with a word in the question or answer choices, try dissecting it. Take advantage of every clue that the word might include. Prefixes and suffixes can be a huge help. Usually they allow you to determine a basic meaning. Pre- means before, post- means after, pro - is positive, de- is negative. From prefixes and suffixes, you can get an idea of the general meaning of the word and try to put it into context.

Hedge Words

Watch out for critical hedge words, such as *likely, may, can, sometimes, often, almost, mostly, usually, generally, rarely,* and *sometimes.* Question writers insert these hedge phrases to cover every possibility. Often an answer choice will be wrong simply because it leaves no room for exception. Be on guard for answer choices that have definitive words such as *exactly* and *always.*

Switchback Words

Stay alert for *switchbacks.* These are the words and phrases frequently used to alert you to shifts in thought. The most common switchback words are *but, although,* and *however.* Others include *nevertheless, on the other hand, even though, while, in spite of, despite, regardless of.* Switchback words are important to catch because they can change the direction of the question or an answer choice.

Face Value

When in doubt, use common sense. Accept the situation in the problem at face value. Don't read too much into it. These problems will not require you to make wild assumptions. If you have to go beyond creativity and warp time or space in order to have an answer choice fit the question, then you should move on and consider the other answer choices. These are normal problems rooted in reality. The applicable relationship or explanation may not be readily apparent, but it is there for you to figure out. Use your common sense to interpret anything that isn't clear.

Answer Choice Strategies

Answer Selection

The most thorough way to pick an answer choice is to identify and eliminate wrong answers until only one is left, then confirm it is the correct answer. Sometimes an answer choice may immediately seem right, but be careful. The test writers will usually put more than one reasonable answer choice on each question, so take a second to read all of them and make sure that the other choices are not equally obvious. As long as you have time left, it is better to read every answer choice than to pick the first one that looks right without checking the others.

Answer Choice Families

An answer choice family consists of two (in rare cases, three) answer choices that are very similar in construction and cannot all be true at the same time. If you see two answer choices that are direct opposites or parallels, one of them is usually the correct answer. For instance, if one answer choice says that quantity x increases and another either says that quantity x decreases (opposite) or says that quantity y increases (parallel), then those answer choices would fall into the same family. An answer choice that doesn't match the construction of the answer choice family is more likely to be incorrect. Most questions will not have answer choice families, but when they do appear, you should be prepared to recognize them.

Eliminate Answers

Eliminate answer choices as soon as you realize they are wrong, but make sure you consider all possibilities. If you are eliminating answer choices and realize that the last one you are left with is also wrong, don't panic. Start over and consider each choice again. There may be something you missed the first time that you will realize on the second pass.

Avoid Fact Traps

Don't be distracted by an answer choice that is factually true but doesn't answer the question. You are looking for the choice that answers the question. Stay focused on what the question is asking for so you don't accidentally pick an answer that is true but incorrect. Always go back to the question and make sure the answer choice you've selected actually answers the question and is not merely a true statement.

Extreme Statements

In general, you should avoid answers that put forth extreme actions as standard practice or proclaim controversial ideas as established fact. An answer choice that states the "process should be used in certain situations, if..." is much more likely to be correct than one that states the "process should be discontinued completely." The first is a calm rational statement and doesn't even make a definitive, uncompromising stance, using a hedge word *if* to provide wiggle room, whereas the second choice is a radical idea and far more extreme.

Benchmark

As you read through the answer choices and you come across one that seems to answer the question well, mentally select that answer choice. This is not your final answer, but it's the one that will help you evaluate the other answer choices. The one that you selected is your benchmark or standard for judging each of the other answer choices. Every other answer choice must be compared to your benchmark. That choice is correct until proven otherwise by another answer choice beating it. If you find a better answer, then that one becomes your new benchmark. Once you've decided that no other choice answers the question as well as your benchmark, you have your final answer.

Predict the Answer

Before you even start looking at the answer choices, it is often best to try to predict the answer. When you come up with the answer on your own, it is easier to avoid distractions and traps because you will know exactly what to look for. The right answer choice is unlikely to be word-for-word what you came up with, but it should be a close match. Even if you are confident that you have the right answer, you should still take the time to read each option before moving on.

General Strategies

Tough Questions

If you are stumped on a problem or it appears too hard or too difficult, don't waste time. Move on! Remember though, if you can quickly check for obviously incorrect answer choices, your chances of guessing correctly are greatly improved. Before you completely give up, at least try to knock out a couple of possible answers. Eliminate what you can and then guess at the remaining answer choices before moving on.

Check Your Work

Since you will probably not know every term listed and the answer to every question, it is important that you get credit for the ones that you do know. Don't miss any questions through careless mistakes. If at all possible, try to take a second to look back over your answer selection and make sure you've selected the correct answer choice and haven't made a costly careless mistake (such as marking an answer choice that you didn't mean to mark). This quick double check should more than pay for itself in caught mistakes for the time it costs.

Pace Yourself

It's easy to be overwhelmed when you're looking at a page full of questions; your mind is confused and full of random thoughts, and the clock is ticking down faster than you would like. Calm down and maintain the pace that you have set for yourself. Especially as you get down to the last few minutes of the test, don't let the small numbers on the clock make you panic. As long as you are on track by monitoring your pace, you are guaranteed to have time for each question.

Don't Rush

It is very easy to make errors when you are in a hurry. Maintaining a fast pace in answering questions is pointless if it makes you miss questions that you would have gotten right otherwise. Test writers like to include distracting information and wrong answers that seem right. Taking a little extra time to avoid careless mistakes can make all the difference in your test score. Find a pace that allows you to be confident in the answers that you select.

Keep Moving

Panicking will not help you pass the test, so do your best to stay calm and keep moving. Taking deep breaths and going through the answer elimination steps you practiced can help to break through a stress barrier and keep your pace.

Final Notes

The combination of a solid foundation of content knowledge and the confidence that comes from practicing your plan for applying that knowledge is the key to maximizing your performance on test day. As your foundation of content knowledge is built up and strengthened, you'll find that the strategies included in this chapter become more and more effective in helping you quickly sift through the distractions and traps of the test to isolate the correct answer.

Now it's time to move on to the test content chapters of this book, but be sure to keep your goal in mind. As you read, think about how you will be able to apply this information on the test. If you've already seen sample questions for the test and you have an idea of the question format and style, try to come up with questions of your own that you can answer based on what you're reading. This will give you valuable practice applying your knowledge in the same ways you can expect to on test day.

Good luck and good studying!

Mathematics

Ratio

A ratio is a direct comparison of two parts of a whole. This is not the same as comparing each part to the whole, as in the case of fractions. For example, for every 3 girls in Maggie's class there are 5 boys. The ratio of girls to boys is a direct comparison of the number of girls and boys, and is therefore 3:5. (Note how this is different from a fraction: 3/8 of the students in Maggie's class are girls, which relates the number of one part, girls, to the whole, students.) Any ratio can be written in three ways: with a colon, as a fraction, or with the word "to". For example, the ratio of girls to boys in Maggie's class can be written as either "3:5", "$\frac{3}{5}$", or "3 to 5". All three ways are read as "three to five".

The following shows how ratios can describe various situations:

- Every car in the parking lot has four wheels. - "Every car in the parking lot has four wheels," means the ratio of cars to wheels is 1:4, because for every one car there are four wheels.
- There are two eyes on every face. - "There are two eyes on every face," means the ratio of eyes to faces is 2:1, because for every two eyes there is one face.
- Every full deck of cards has four aces. - "Every full deck of cards has four aces," means either that the ratio of decks to aces is 1:4, because for each deck there are four aces, or that the ratio of cards to aces is 52:4, because for every set of 52 cards (1 deck), there are 4 aces.
- A recipe calls for two cups of flour for every two dozen cookies. - "A recipe calls for two cups of flour for every two dozen cookies," means the ratio of cups of flour to cookies is 2:24, because for every two cups of flour used 24 (two dozen) cookies will be made.

Unit rate

Unit rate expresses a quantity of one thing in terms of one unit of another. For example, if you travel 30 miles every two hours, a unit rate expresses this comparison in terms of one hour: in one hour you travel 15 miles, so your unit rate is 15 miles per hour. Other examples are how much one ounce of food costs (price per ounce), or figuring out how much one egg costs out of the dozen (price per 1 egg, instead of price per 12 eggs). The denominator of a unit rate is always 1. Unit rates are used to compare different situations to solve problems. For example, to make sure you get the best deal when deciding which kind of soda to buy, you can find the unit rate of each. If Soda #1 costs $1.50 for a 1-liter bottle, and soda #2 costs $2.75 for a 2-liter bottle, it would be a better deal to buy Soda #2, because its unit rate is only $1.375 per 1-liter, which is cheaper than Soda #1. Unit rates can also help determine the length of time a given event will take. For example, if you can paint 2 rooms in 4.5 hours, you can determine how long it will take you to paint 5 rooms by solving for the unit rate per room and then multiplying that by 5.

Example problem 1

At the store you see two different bags of candy for sale. Bag A has 32 pieces of candy in it and costs $2.10. Bag B has 50 pieces of candy in it and costs $3.50. Find the unit cost per one piece of candy from each bag and determine which is the better deal.

One piece of candy in Bag A costs about $0.065, or 6.5 cents. This can be found be taking the total price, $2.10, and dividing it by the number of pieces of candy, 32, to determine the cost for one piece of candy: $\frac{2.10}{32} = 0.06562$, or about $0.065. One piece of candy in Bag B costs $0.07, or 7 cents. This can be found in the same way, dividing the total cost, $3.50, by the number of pieces of candy, 50: $\frac{3.5}{50} = 0.07$, or $0.07. Since a piece of candy in Bag B is slightly more expensive, it is the better deal to buy Bag A.

Example problem 2

You decide to bake oatmeal cookies for a bake sale. Your recipe calls for 5 cups of flour, 2 cups of sugar, 1 cup of butter, and 3 cups of oats. However, you only have 1 cup of oats. You decide to make as many cookies as you can with the 1 cup of oats that you have. Find how much of each ingredient you will need to make that many cookies.

You will need to use $1\,^2/_3$ cups of flour, $^2/_3$ cup of sugar, and $^1/_3$ cup of butter. These can be found by finding the unit rate of each per 1 cup of oats. If there are 5 cups of flour needed for every 3 cups of oats, then $\frac{5}{3} = 1\,^2/_3$ cups of flour needed for every 1 cup of oats. Similarly, if there needs to be 2 cups of sugar for every 3 cups of oats, then there needs to be $^2/_3$ cup of sugar for every 1 cup of oats. And finally, if there is 1 cup of butter needed for every 3 cups of oats, then there will need to be $^1/_3$ cup of butter for every 1 cup of oats.

- 13 -

Example problem 3

Janice made $40 during the first 5 hours she spent babysitting. She will continue to earn money at this rate until she finishes babysitting in 3 more hours. Find how much money Janice earned babysitting and how much she earns per hour.

Janice will earn $64 babysitting in her 8 total hours (adding the first 5 hours to the remaining 3 gives the 8 hour total). This can be found by setting up a proportion comparing money earned to babysitting hours. Since she earns $40 for 5 hours and since the rate is constant, she will earn a proportional amount in 8 hours: $\frac{40}{5} = \frac{x}{8}$. Cross-multiplying will yield $5x = 320$, and division by 5 shows that $x = 64$.

Janice earns $8 per hour. This can be found by taking her total amount earned, $64, and dividing it by the total number of hours worked, 8. Since $\frac{64}{8} = 8$, Janice makes $8 in one hour. This can also be found by finding the unit rate, money earned per hour: $\frac{64}{8} = \frac{x}{1}$. Since cross-multiplying yields $8x = 64$, and division by 8 shows that $x = 8$, Janice earns $8 per hour.

Example problem 4

The McDonalds are taking a family road trip, driving 300 miles to their cabin. It took them 2 hours to drive the first 120 miles. They will drive at the same speed all the way to their cabin. Find the speed at which the McDonalds are driving and how much longer it will take them to get to their cabin.

The McDonalds are driving 60 miles per hour. This can be found by setting up a proportion to find the unit rate, the number of miles they drive per one hour: $\frac{120}{2} = \frac{x}{1}$. Cross-multiplying yields $2x = 120$ and division by 2 shows that $x = 60$.

Since the McDonalds will drive this same speed, it will take them another 3 hours to get to their cabin. This can be found by first finding how many miles the McDonalds have left to drive, which is 300 – 120 = 180. The McDonalds are driving at 60 miles per hour, so a proportion can be set up to determine how many hours it will take them to drive 180 miles: $\frac{180}{x} = \frac{60}{1}$. Cross-multiplying yields $60x = 180$, and division by 60 shows that $x = 3$. This can also be found by using the formula $D = r \times t$ (or $Distance = rate \times time$), where $180 = 60 \times t$, and division by 60 shows that $t = 3$.

Example problem 5

It takes Andy 10 minutes to read 6 pages of his book. He has already read 150 pages in his book that is 210 pages long. Find how long it takes Andy to read 1 page and also find how long it will take him to finish his book if he continues to read at the same speed.

It takes Andy 1 minute and 40 seconds to read one page in his book. This can be found by finding the unit rate per one page, by dividing the total time it takes him to read 6 pages by 6. Since it takes him 10 minutes to read 6 pages, $\frac{10}{6} = 1\,^2/_3$ minutes, which is 1 minute and 40 seconds.

It will take Andy another 100 minutes, or 1 hour and 40 minutes to finish his book. This can be found by first figuring out how many pages Andy has left to read, which is 210-150 = 60. Since it is now known that it takes him $1\,^2/_3$ minutes to read each page, then that rate must be multiplied by however many pages he has left to read (60) to find the time he'll need: $60 \times 1\,^2/_3 = 100$, so it will take him 100 minutes, or 1 hour and 40 minutes, to read the rest of his book.

Example problem 6

Find the unit rate in the situations given:
   A. *Pizza Place is offering a deal for $40 for 8 pizzas. What is the cost of each pizza?*
   B. *The ratio of flight attendants to airplanes is 42:14. How many flight attendants are on each airplane?*
   C. *Milo has a pledge of $100 for the 25 mile walk-a-thon. How much will Milo earn for each mile?*
   D. *It takes the cleaning service 8 hours to clean 20 garages. How long does it take to clean 1 garage?*

A. The unit rate is $5 per pizza. This is found by $\frac{\$40}{8} = \$5$.

B. The unit ratio is 3:1 which means there are 3 flight attendants for each airplane. This is found by $\frac{42}{14} = 3$.

C. The unit rate is $4 per mile. This is found by $\frac{\$100}{25} = \$4$.

D. The unit rate is 0.4 hours, or 24 minutes, to clean one garage. This is found by $\frac{8\ hours}{20} = 0.4$ hours. This can be converted to minutes multiplying by a conversion factor: $0.4\ hours \times \frac{60\ minutes}{1\ hour} = 24\ minutes$.

Percent

Percent is one way of expressing what portion something is out of a whole. You can think of it like dividing the whole into 100 equal parts, called percents. The whole, all 100 parts, is called 100% (read as "one hundred percent"). Half of the whole is half (50) of the parts, so we say it is 50%, and so on. (Percent compares one quantity to another; sometimes neither number is necessarily 'whole' or 'all' of something.) To find what percent one number is of another, divide the first by the second, and multiply the answer by 100. For example, we can use percent to compare a part to a whole by asking how much money someone spends on their housing payment each month out of his or her total amount of money that month. If someone earns $2000 every month and spends $800 of that on their housing payment, then that person spends $\frac{800}{2000} \times (100) = 0.4 \times 100 = 40\%$ of his or her income on housing payments. Another example showing how percent can simply relate two numbers is comparing your age to your mother's age. If you are 12 years old and your mother is 40 years old, then you are $\frac{12}{40} \times 100 = 0.3 \times 100 = 30\%$ of her age.

Example problem 1

Johnny got 80% of the questions correct on his math test. Find how many questions Johnny answered correctly if the test had 75 questions on it. Also, find what Johnny's new score would be if he was able to earn an extra 10% of his original score by doing corrections on the questions he missed.

Johnny got 60 questions correct. To find this, set up the percent calculation, leaving the number Johnny got right as x: $(\frac{x}{75} \times 100 = 80\%$. Multiply both sides by 75 and then divide both sides by 100 to solve for $x = \frac{80 \times 75}{100} = 60$. We say we are finding 80% of 75, which we now know means simply multiplying 75 by 0.80, which is 60.

Johnny's new score would be $^{66}/_{75}$, which is a score of 88%. This can be found in two ways. One is finding what number of questions is 10% of Johnny's original number right, or 10% of 60, which is 6 questions. If Johnny gets those 6 questions added back to his score, he would then have a total of 66 questions correct out of 75, which is $\frac{66}{75}$, which is 0.88, or 88%. The other way is by finding 10% of Johnny's original score of 80% and adding that to his original score: 10% of 80% = 0.10 × 80% = 8%, and 80% + 8% = 88%.

Example problem 2

A sweater at a local department store is on sale for $33. Find the original price of the sweater if it is marked 40% off the original price.

The sweater was originally $55. To find this, set up a proportion to determine what number 33 is 60% of. We use 60% because if the sweater is 40% *off* we *subtracted* 40% from the price, so we have 60% *left*. The proportion will compare the percent over 100 to 33 over the original price: $\frac{60}{100} = \frac{33}{x}$. Cross-multiplying yields $60x = 3300$, and division by 60 shows that $x = 55$.

Greater or equal to

<u>Examples</u>

For each situation listed below, determine which quantity is greater or if they are equal:

3 yards and 20 feet

70 minutes and 1 hour

188 pennies and 2 dollars

2 feet and 24 inches

1 kilometer and 100 meters

> 20 feet is greater. Since there are 3 feet in each yard, there are 9 feet in 3 yards, and 20 feet is greater than 9 feet.
>
> 70 minutes is greater, since there are only 60 minutes in one hour.
>
> 2 dollars is greater. Since there are 100 pennies in each dollar, there are 200 pennies in 2 dollars, which is greater than 188 pennies.
>
> These quantities are equal, since there are 12 inches in each foot, and therefore 24 inches in 2 feet.
>
> 1 kilometer is greater, because in each kilometer there are 1000 meters, which is greater than 100 meters.

Conversions

<u>Example problem 1</u>

> *Tony is going to buy new carpet for two rooms in his house. One room is $12\ feet \times 12\ feet$, and the other is $10\ feet \times 18\ feet$. The carpet Tony wants to buy is on sale for $10 per square yard. How much will Tony pay for the amount of carpet he needs for both rooms?*
>
> Tony will pay $360 for his carpet. First figure out how much carpet Tony needs to buy in square yards and then multiply that by $10 per square yard.
>
> Since Tony's room dimensions are in feet, they must first be converted to yards. The first room is 12 feet × 12 feet, and since there are 3 feet in each yard, that room is 4 yards × 4 yards (because $\frac{12}{3} = 4$). Similarly, the room that is 10 feet × 18 feet measures $3\frac{1}{3}$ yards × 6 yards (because $\frac{10}{3} = 3\frac{1}{3}$, and $\frac{18}{3} = 6$). So, the total square yardage of Tony's rooms is $4 \times 4 = 16$ square yards, plus $3\frac{1}{3} \times 6 = 20$ square yards, or 16 + 20 = 36 square yards. Since the carpet costs $10 per square yard, then the total cost is $10 \times 36 = \$360$.

Example problem 2

Tyson is driving home from work. He is driving 45 miles per hour and is 10 miles away from home. Find how many minutes it will take Tyson to get the rest of the way home if he continues to drive at the same speed.

It will take Tyson $13\frac{1}{3}$ minutes to get home. Convert Tyson's speed to miles per minute, using a conversion factor of 60 minutes in 1 hour: $\frac{45\ miles}{1\ hour} \times \frac{1\ hour}{60\ minutes} =$ $0.75\ ^{miles}/_{minute}$. (The 'hours' units cancel and the answer is then in 'miles per minute'.) Because $distance = rate \times time$, $\frac{distance}{rate} = time$. Therefore, if Tyson has 10 miles left to go, dividing that by 0.75 miles per minute finds how many minutes it will take Tyson to get home. $\frac{10}{0.75} = 13\frac{1}{3}$, so it will take Tyson $13\frac{1}{3}$ minutes to get home.

Example problem 3

When Mrs. Smith turned 50 years old she wanted to figure out how many minutes she had been alive. She determined that she had been alive for 25,000,000 minutes. Is she correct?

No, Mrs. Smith is not correct. She has been alive for 26,280,000 minutes. This is found by converting 50 years into minutes, using conversion factors from years to days to hours to minutes: $50\ years \times \frac{365\ days}{1\ year} \times \frac{24\ hours}{1\ day} \times \frac{60\ minutes}{1\ hour} = 26{,}280{,}000$ minutes. The first multiplication operation will give 18,250, which is how many days Mrs. Smith has been alive (the 'years' units cancel). Multiplying that by $\frac{24\ hours}{1\ day}$ will cancel the 'days' units and yield 438,000 hours. Finally, multiplying that by $\frac{60\ minutes}{1\ hour}$ will cancel the 'hours' units and leave an answer of 26,280,000 minutes.

- 18 -

Division

Example problem

Solve the following division problem:

$$9\overline{)9027}$$

The answer to the problem of 9027 divided by 9 is 1003.

$$
\begin{array}{r}
1003 \\
9\overline{)9027} \\
9000 \\
\hline
0027 \\
0027 \\
\hline
0
\end{array}
$$

Of course, 9 divides into 9 exactly one time, so a 1 is placed on the answer line, and the product of 1 and 9 is placed under the thousands place of the dividend. (The remaining places are zero). 9 does not go into 0, so a 0 is placed on the answer line above 0. Since 9 also does not go into 2, another 0 is placed on the answer line. 9 goes into 27 three times, so a 3 is placed on the answer line above the 7. There is no remainder, because 9 goes into 27 exactly 3 times with nothing left over.

Decimals

Example problem 1

Add the following decimals:

13.48

+2.5

The answer is 15.98.

13.48

+2.5

15.98

It is important to line up the digits correctly which can be done by making sure that the decimal points are lined up vertically, which results in lining up digits that have the same place values. Start by putting a decimal point in the answer line directly below the decimal points in the problem, and then add the digits in the column farthest to the right. There is no digit in 2.5 that lines up with the 8 in 13.48, so 0 is added to 8, and the answer, 8, is brought down below the addition line to the answer. Next, add the 4 and 5, as they are in the same place value (the tenths place in this case); put their sum, 9, in the tenths place of the answer. Adding the digits in the ones place puts a 5 in the ones place of the answer.

Finally, the 1 in the tens place in 13.48 isn't added to any digit in 2.5, so the sum of 1 and 0 is put in the tens place of the answer, which makes the final answer 15.98.

Example problem 2

Subtract the following decimals:

37.4

- 5.32

The answer is 32.08.

37.4

- 5.32

32.08

It is important to line up the digits correctly which can be done by making sure that the decimal points are lined up vertically, which results in lining up digits that have the same place values. Start by putting a decimal point in the answer line directly below the decimal points in the problem, and then subtract the digits in the column farthest to the right, the top minus the bottom. Since there is currently no digit above the 2, it is considered a 0, but since 2 cannot be subtracted from 0, borrow from the 4, making the 0 a 10 and making the 4 a 3. Since 2 can now be subtracted from 10, put the answer, 8, in the hundredths place of the answer. Now subtract 3 (remember: it's not a 4 anymore!) from 3, which is 0. In the ones place subtract 5 from 7, which is 2. And finally nothing is being subtracted from the 3 in the tens place in 37.4, so the 3 is brought down to the answer, making the final answer 32.08.

Prime factorization

Prime Factorization is breaking a number down into a list of its prime factors. For example, the prime factorization of 60 is $2 \times 2 \times 3 \times 5$, because 2, 3, and 5 are all prime numbers and $2 \times 2 \times 3 \times 5 = 60$. This can be found by first breaking down 60 into any two factors, perhaps 30 and 2. Since 2 is a prime number, it's already a prime factor, but 30 needs to be broken down into factors. 30 can be broken into 2 and 15, 3 and 10, or 6 and 5, but it does not matter which we use. If 3 and 10 are used, the factorization of 60 is $2 \times 3 \times 10$. Since 2 and 3 are prime but 10 is not, we have to break 10 down into 2 and 5, which now makes the factorization of 60 = $2 \times 3 \times 2 \times 5$. This is the prime factorization of 60 because these numbers are all prime. To report the answer in proper form put the numbers in order from least to greatest: the final answer for the prime factorization of 60 is $2 \times 2 \times 3 \times 5$.

Greatest common factor

The greatest common factor is the greatest number that all numbers in a set are evenly divisible by. For example, the Greatest Common Factor of 36 and 48 is 12. One way to find this is by simply listing all the factors of 36 and 48; the common factors of 36 and 48 are 1, 2, 3, 4, 6, and 12, and 12 is the greatest of these. This can also be found using the prime factorization of both 36 and 48. The prime factorization of 36 is $2 \times 2 \times 3 \times 3$, and the prime factorization of 48 is $2 \times 2 \times 2 \times 2 \times 3$. Find how many of each prime factor these factorizations have in common: both factorizations have two 2's and one 3, so the Greatest Common Factor of 36 and 48 must be $2 \times 2 \times 3$, which equals 12.

<u>Examples</u>

The following sums can be expressed by factoring out a common factor:

15 + 21
16 + 20
50 + 80
27 + 63
6 + 52
18 + 66

'15 + 21' = 3(5 + 7)

'16 + 20' = 4(4 + 5)

'50 + 80' = 10(5 + 8)

'27 + 63' = 9(3 + 7)

'6 + 52' = 2(3 + 26)

'18 + 66' = 6(3 + 11)

These answers cannot be factored any further because there are no common factors left between the numbers inside the parentheses. In other words, the number that was factored out of each pair of numbers is that pair's greatest common factor.

Least common multiple

The least common multiple is the smallest number that is evenly divisible by all numbers in a given set. For example, the least common multiple of 6 and 8 is 24. One way to find this is to list the common multiples of 6 and 8, 24, 48, 72, ...etc, and the least of these is 24. This can also be found using the prime factorization of both 6 and 8. The prime factorization of 6 is 2×3, and the prime factorization of 8 is $2 \times 2 \times 2$. For each factor, count the number of times it occurs in each factorization. Find the greatest number of times each factor shows up, and multiply each factor that many times. Since 2 shows up three times in 8's factorization, and 3 shows up once in 6's prime factorization, multiply $2 \times 2 \times 2 \times 3$, which equals 24.

Highest and lowest temperature

Example problem

At 1am in Anchorage, Alaska, it was -17°outside. The temperature fell a total of 10 degrees by sunrise, and then rose steadily a total of 35 degrees until 1pm, when the highest temperature of the day occurred. Find the lowest temperature during the night and the warmest temperature of the day.

> The lowest temperature during the night was -27° and the warmest temperature of the day was 8°. Since the temperature falls 10° from -17°, subtract 10 from -17: -17 -10 = -27, and the lowest temperature was -27°. From this lowest temperature it rises a total 35° which brings the thermometer up to 8° because -27 + 35 = 8. This can be thought of in two ways: first, because of the commutative property, -27 + 35 = 35 + -27, which is the same as 35 – 27, which equals 8. The other way is to recognize that the temperature must rise 27 degrees from -27° to get to 0°, but we know it rises another 8°, because the difference between 35 and 27 is 8.

Variables, numbers, and operation symbols

Examples

Use variables, numbers, and operation symbols to express the following:

3 less than a number n
The quotient of 4 and a number x
The difference between 10 and y
The product of 12 and m
The sum of x and 4
6 more than a number r

> "3 less than a number n" means taking 3 away from the value of n, so this is expressed as $n - 3$.

> "The quotient of 4 and a number x" means dividing 4 by x, so we write $\frac{4}{x}$.

> "The difference between 10 and y" means subtracting y from 10, so we write $10 - y$.

> "The product of 12 and m" means multiplying 12 and m, so we write $12 \times m$, or simply $12m$.

> "The sum of x and 4" means adding x and 4, so we write $x +\_4$.

> "6 more than a number r" means adding 6 to r, so we write $r +6$.

Addition and subtraction with positives and negatives

Example problem 1

On Monday of last week, Molly's credit card had a balance of $50 owing on it. Throughout the week Molly made new charges on her credit card when she spent $75 at the grocery store on Tuesday, $30 on a haircut on Wednesday, and $15 at the movies on Friday. On Saturday she made a payment of $200 to her credit card

- 22 -

and then on Sunday made another charge of $40 to buy new shoes. Determine whether Molly's credit card has a balance on Sunday night, and if so, how much it is.

> Molly's credit card has a balance of $10 on Sunday night. This can be found by subtracting Molly's charges and adding her payment to her balance. A charge on a credit card, or balance, is a negative number because it is owed to the credit card company. A payment on the card gives the company money they are owed, so it is a positive number added to the balance to make that balance *less* negative. In Molly's case, she starts the week with a $50 balance, which is like starting with -50. The three charges on Tuesday, Wednesday, and Friday need to be subtracted from this, to get $-50 - 75 - 30 - 15 = -170$. When Molly makes a payment of $200, then, she only owed $170 on her credit card, so that -170 + 200 = positive 30. (Positive balances are money the company owes to Molly!) After that she makes another charge of $40, which is subtracted from 30 to get a final amount of -10. This means that at the end of the week Molly owes her credit card company $10, and we say her credit card has a balance of $10.

Example problem 2

A helicopter is flying directly above a submarine. The submarine travels to 600 feet below sea level, while the helicopter reaches its flying height of 1050 feet. Find how far away the submarine and helicopter are from each other.

> The helicopter and submarine are 1650 feet apart. This is found by adding their distances to sea level, because we can think of sea level as a value of zero in this situation. The helicopter is 1050 feet above sea level, which is like +1050, and its distance to sea level, 0, is 1050 feet. The submarine is 600 feet below sea level, which is like -600, and the distance from the submarine to sea level is 600 feet. The total distance between the helicopter and submarine, then, is 1050 + 600 = 1650 feet.

Properties

Example problem 1

State which property is being used in each number sentence:

$$2x + y = y + 2x$$
$$5 \times (x + 1) = (5 \times x) + (5 \times 1)$$
$$3 \times 1 = 3$$
$$6 \times m \times n = m \times n \times 6$$
$$4 \times (5a) = (4a) \times 5$$
$$s + 0 = s$$
$$10 + (6 + 1) = (10 + 6) + 1$$

The Commutative Property of Addition is shown here, which states that you can add terms in any order.

The Distributive Property is shown here, which states that a number multiplied to an expression in parentheses must be multiplied to every term in the parentheses.

The Identity Property of Multiplication is shown here, which states that multiplying a number or term by 1 does not change its value.

The Commutative Property of Multiplication is shown here, which states that you can multiply terms in any order.

The Associative Property of Multiplication is shown here, which states that any group of numbers and/or variables can be grouped together in parentheses to be multiplied first before multiplying by the remaining numbers and/or variables.

"$s + 0 = s$" – The Identity Property of Addition is shown here, which states that adding 0 to any number or term does not change the value of that number or term.

The Associative Property of Addition is shown here, which states that any group of numbers and/or variables can be grouped together in parentheses to be added first before adding the remaining numbers and/or variables.

Example problem 2

Simplify the following expressions and state what property, or properties, you used:

    A. $3(2x - 1)$
    B. $4x + y + 2x - 3y$
    C. $2(5 + m) - 2m$
    D. $7(2x)$

A. This simplifies to "$6x - 3$". The multiplication by 3 has to be distributed to both terms in the parentheses, which is the Distributive Property.
B. This simplifies to "$6x - 2y$", since combining like terms by adding them first ($4x + 2x = 6x$) and then adding those sums uses the Commutative Property of Addition.
C. This simplifies to 10. This is done using the Distributive Property to first multiply the 2 to each term in the parentheses to get "$10 + 2m - 2m$" and then combining like terms, using the Commutative Property of Addition. Since the like terms in this case are a positive $2m$ and a negative $2m$, they add to zero and therefore the answer is simply 10.
D. This simplifies to "$14x$" using the Associative Property of Multiplication.

Example problem 3

Use the distributive property to match one expression in Column I with an equivalent expression in Column II.

Column I	Column II
A. 4(3x-1)	U. 10x+25y
B. 8(9+2x)	V. 12x-4
C. 36-2x	W. 3(4x-8y)
D. 4(4a+5)	X. 72+16x
E. 12x-24y	Y. 2(18-x)
F. 5(2x+5y)	Z. 16a+20

- A is equivalent to V, by distributing the '4' into the parentheses.
- B is equivalent to X by distributing the '8' into the parentheses.
- C is equivalent to Y by distributing the '2' in Y back into the parentheses, or by factoring 2 from both the '36' and the '$2x$'.
- D is equivalent to Z by distributing the '4' into the parentheses.
- E is equivalent to W by distributing the '3' in W back into the parentheses, or by factoring '3' from both the '$12x$' and '$24y$'.
- F is equivalent to U by distributing the '5' into the parentheses.

Proportions

Example problem 1

Using the table below, find the values of a and b.

Gallons of Gas	Price in Dollars
2	a
5	20
b	32
9	36

The value of a is 8 and the value of b is also 8. They can both be found by setting up proportions. To find the value of a, a proportion can be set up comparing 2 and a with the values in the second row, 5 and 20: $\frac{2}{a} = \frac{5}{20}$. Cross multiplying yields $40 = 5a$, and division by 5 shows that $a = 8$.

To find the value of b, another proportion can be set up, comparing b and 32 with any other pair of data in the table. Using 9 and 36 yields the proportion $\frac{b}{32} = \frac{9}{36}$, and cross multiplying yields $36b = 288$. Division by 36 shows that $b = 8$.

Example problem 2

Using the tables comparing Janaya's and Tim's running speeds, decide who will win a race that is 100 meters long.

Janaya

Distance	Time
10m	1.4 seconds
45m	6.3 seconds
85m	11.9 seconds

Tim

Distance	Time
12m	1.8 seconds
50m	7.5 seconds
85m	11.25 seconds

Janaya will win a 100m race against Tim, because Janaya will run 100m in 14 seconds, and Tim will run 100m in 15 seconds. Set up proportions to solve for what each runner's time will be for a 100m distance. To solve for Janaya's time, we can compare 100m with the unknown time, x, to any other pair of data in her table. If we use 10m and 1.4 seconds, the proportion $\frac{10}{1.4} = \frac{100}{x}$ yields $10x = 140$ after cross-multiplication and division by 10 yields $x = 14$. To solve for Tim's time, we can compare 100m with his unknown time, y, to any other pair of data in his table. If we use 50m and 7.5 seconds, the proportion $\frac{50}{7.5} = \frac{100}{y}$ will give $50y = 750$ and division by 50 will give $y = 15$. Since it will take Tim 1 second longer, Janaya will win.

Coordinate plane

Four quadrants and the range of x and y-values

The four quadrants in a coordinate plane are called Quadrant I, Quadrant II, Quadrant III, and Quadrant IV. Quadrant I is the upper right quadrant of the plane and contains ordered pairs where $x > 0$ and $y > 0$. Quadrant II is the upper left quadrant of the plane and contains ordered pairs where $x < 0$ and $y > 0$. Quadrant III is the lower left quadrant of the plane and contains ordered pairs where $x < 0$ and $y < 0$.

Quadrant IV is the lower right quadrant of the plane and contains ordered pairs where $x > 0$ and $y < 0$. The coordinate plane below shows the four quadrants:

Example problem 1

Plot the data in the table below on a coordinate plane and find the value of y when $x = 1$.

X	Y
-4	-1
-2	1
0	3
2	5

Pairs of values (x, y) in the table are plotted on the coordinate plane below:

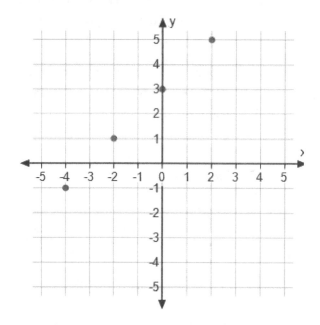

The value of y is 4 when $x = 1$. This can be found by looking at the graph or the table to determine what the pattern of the data is and where the point would lie when $x = 1$. The pattern in the graph and table is that y increases at a rate of 1 vertically for every 1 horizontally; in other words, for every time x increases by 1, y increases by 1 also. It can then be determined that since the y-value was 3 when the x-value was 0, the y-value will be 4 when the x-value is 1.

Example problem 2

Plot the following points in a coordinate plane and describe each point's location:

Point A: (5, 0)
Point B: (-2, 2)
Point C: (-3, -1)
Point D: (3, 1)
Point E: (0, 0)
Point F: (0, -4)
Point G: (2, -3)

The graph below shows the location of the points:

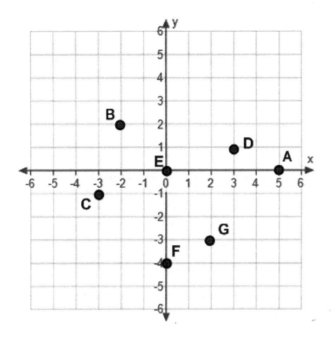

Point A is located on the $x - axis$, 5 units to the right of the origin. Point B is located in Quadrant II, 2 units to the left of the origin and 2 units up. Point C is located in Quadrant III, 3 units to the left of the origin and 1 unit down. Point D is located in Quadrant I, 3 units to the right of the origin and 1 unit up. Point E is located at the origin. Point F is located on the $y-axis$, 4 units down from the origin. Point G is located in Quadrant IV, 2 units to the right of the origin and 3 units down.

Example problem 3

Find the perimeter of the rectangle in the coordinate plane below using the values of the coordinates of the vertices:

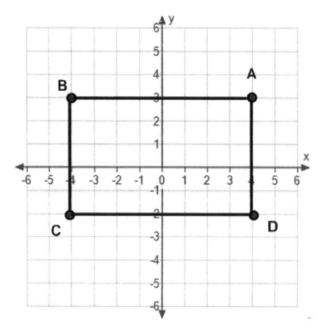

The perimeter of the rectangle is 26 units. This can be found by first finding the ordered pairs of each vertex of the rectangle, which are A= (4, 3), B= (-4, 3), C= (-4, -2), and D= (4, -2), and then using these to find the lengths of the four sides of the rectangle. Since each consecutive pair of vertices share either the same $x-$ coordinate or $y-$ coordinate, it is only necessary to consider the coordinates that are different in value. The distances from A to B and from C to D are each 8, which can be found by finding the distance between their $x-$ coordinates. The distance between 4 and -4 is 8, because 4 is 4 units away from zero and -4 is also 4 units away from zero which gives a total length of $4 + 4 = 8$. The distance from B to C and from D to A are each 5, which can be found by finding the distance between their $y-$ coordinates. The distance between 3 and -2 is 5, because 3 is 3 units away from zero and -2 is 2 units away from zero which gives a total length of $3 + 2 = 5$. Therefore the total perimeter of the rectangle is $8 + 8 + 5 + 5 = 26$ units.

- 28 -

Example problem 4

Find the remaining ordered pairs of the vertices of a square in the coordinate plane below if one side length of the square is 5 units and it has a vertex in each quadrant.

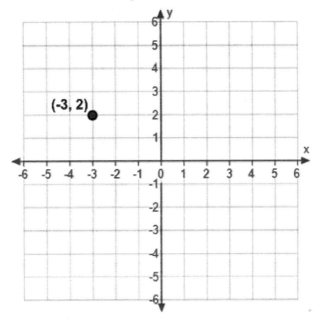

The remaining vertices have the ordered pairs of (-3, -3), (2, -3), and (2, 2). This is found by first figuring out what point in Quadrant III is 5 units away from the given point. It will have the same x −coordinate, so the value of y needs to be 5 units away from 2. Going 2 units away from 2 gets to 0, and then 3 more units must be traveled, getting to the point (-3, -3). Then figure out what point in Quadrant IV is 5 units away from (-3, -3). It will have the same y −coordinate, so the value of x needs to be 5 units away from -3. Going 3 units to the right of -3 gets to 0, and then 2 more units must be traveled, getting to the point (2, -3). Finally figure out what point in Quadrant I is 5 units away from (2, -3). It will have the same x −coordinate as the point in Quadrant IV, and the same y-coordinate as the point in Quadrant II, so the point must be (2, 2). This can be verified: the value of y needs to be 5 units away from -3. Going 3 units away from -3 gets to 0, and then 2 more units must be traveled, getting to the point (2, 2).

Coordinate grid

Example problem 1

Your neighborhood can be represented by a coordinate grid, with each unit representing 1 block. Your house is located at (1,5), the park is located at (5,5), the drug store is located at (5,0), and the gas station is located at (1,0). Each morning you go for a run from your house along a route to the park, then the drug store, the gas station, and then back home. Plot this route on a coordinate grid and determine how many blocks you run.

You run 18 blocks on this route:

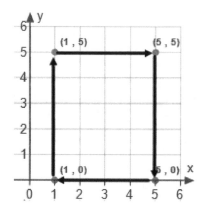

With each dot representing a location in your neighborhood, the route forms a rectangle. The first part of the route is 4 blocks to get from your house to the park, then 5 blocks to get from the park to the drug store, 4 more blocks to get from the drug store to the gas station, and finally 5 blocks to get from the gas station back to your house. Adding all these together gives you $4 + 5 + 4 + 5 = 18$ blocks. These distances can be found by either counting the number of squares on the grid between each location, or by finding the distance between the x or y coordinates (depending whether you're moving horizontally or vertically on the graph, respectively) of two points. For example, the distance between your house at (1,5) and the park at (5,5) is $5 - 1 = 4$ blocks, because you need to go 4 blocks over to get from the x-coordinate of 1 to the x-coordinate of 5, while not moving y-coordinates at all.

Example problem 2

Platt Middle School was designed using a coordinate grid with each unit of measure representing 1 block. In the school, the library is located at (1, 4), the cafeteria is located at (-3, 4) and the gym is located at (1, -2).

- 30 -

Plot these points on a coordinate grid and find the shortest distance a student needs to walk to get from gym class to the library and then to lunch.

The student will need to walk 10 blocks. This can be found by first finding the distance from the gym at (1, -2) to the library at (1, 4), and then the library to the cafeteria at (-3, 4). To get from the gym to the library the student will need to walk along a straight path along the x-coordinate of 1, from y-coordinates -2 to 4. The distance -2 is from 0 is 2, and the distance 4 is from 0 is 4. Therefore, the student must walk $2 + 4 = 6$ blocks from the gym to the library. Then the student will walk in a straight path along the y-coordinate of 4 from x-coordinates 1 to -3. The distance 1 is from 0 is 1, and the distance -3 is from 0 is 3. Therefore, the student must walk $1 + 3 = 4$ blocks from the library to lunch in the cafeteria. Thus, the student must walk a total of $6 + 4 = 10$ blocks to get from the gym to the library and then to lunch. The graph below shows the location of the places in the school and the student's path:

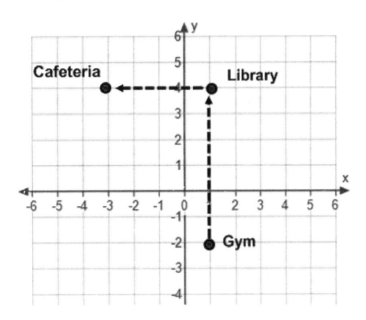

Example problem 3

The downtown area of Cannonville has streets that follow a coordinate grid. The mayor is planning a parade through downtown and the city council has limited the length of the parade to 16 blocks. The mayor wants the parade to travel from the Zoo at (-5, -4) to the Park at (-3, -4), to the Bakery at (-3, 1), to the Library at (-1, 1), to the Post Office at (-1, -1), to City Hall at (2, -1), and ending at the Town Square at (2, 2). Plot this proposed route of the parade on a coordinate plane and determine if it will fit the requirement of the city council.

The distance of the proposed parade is 17 blocks so it will not make the 16 block requirement from the city council. This distance can be found by determining the distance between each pair of consecutive parade locations. Since each pair of consecutive locations share either an x or y −coordinate, the distance is found by calculating the distance between the different coordinates. When finding the distance between coordinates of opposite signs, first find the absolute value of each, which gives the distance of each from 0, and add them together. The distances are: **1.** Zoo to Park is 2 blocks, which is the distance between x −coordinates -5 and -3. **2.** Park to Bakery is 5 blocks, which is the distance between y-coordinates -4 and 1 because $|-4| + |1| = 5$. **3.** Bakery to the Library is 2 blocks, which is the distance between x −coordinates -3 and -1. **4.** Library to

- 31 -

Post Office is 2 blocks, which is the distance between y-coordinates 1 and -1 because $|-1| + |1| = 2$. **5.** Post Office to City Hall is 3 blocks, which is the distance between x-coordinates -1 and 2 because $|-1| + |2| = 3$. **6.** City Hall to Town Square is 3 blocks, which is the distance between y-coordinates -1 and 2 because $|-1| + |2| = 3$. **7.** The total distance is then $2 + 5 + 2 + 2 + 3 + 3 = 17$.

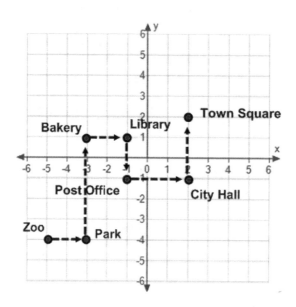

Reflections

Example problem 1

Label the following points and their indicated reflections in a coordinate plane and give the coordinates of the reflections:

Point A: (4, 3) reflected across the $x - axis$
Point B: (1, 2) reflected across the $y - axis$
Point C: (-2, -5) reflected across the $y - axis$
Point D: (3, 1) reflected across the $x - axis$ and then the $y - axis$

The graph below shows the points and their reflections:

- The reflection of Point A is labeled as A' and has coordinates (4, -3). Because it is reflected across the $x - axis$, the $y - value$ changes in sign.
- The reflection of Point B is labeled as B' and has coordinates (-1, 2). Because it is reflected across the $y - axis$, the $x - value$ changes in sign.
- The reflection of Point C is labeled as C' and has coordinates (2, -5). Because it is reflected across the $y - axis$, the $x - value$ changes in sign.
- The reflection of Point D is labeled as D' and has coordinates (-3, -1). Because it is reflected across both the x and $y - axes$, both the x and $y - values$ change in sign.

- 32 -

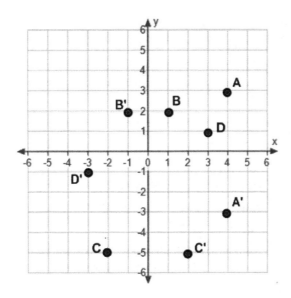

Example problem 2

Identify the reflections that produce the second of each pair from the first of each pair:

(2, 6) and (-2, 6)
(-4, 0) and (4, 0)
(-1, -1) and (-1, 1)
(5, -7) and (-5, 7)

The reflection from (2, 6) to (-2, 6) is a reflection across the $y-axis$. This is because the $x-value$ has changed in sign.

The reflection from (-4, 0) to (4, 0) is a reflection across the $y-axis$. This is because the $x-value$ has changed in sign.

The reflection from (-1, -1) to (-1, 1) is a reflection across the $x-axis$. This is because the $y-value$ has changed in sign.

The reflection from (5, -7) to (-5, 7) is a reflection across both the x and $y-axis$. This is because both the x and $y-values$ have changed in sign.

Fractions

Example problem 1

You and your best friend plan to split the remaining amount of a large pizza. If there is $\frac{3}{4}$ of the pizza left, find what fraction of the original pizza each of you will get and represent the solution with a diagram.

You each get $\frac{3}{8}$ of the original pizza. This is found by dividing $\frac{3}{4}$ by 2. When dividing with fractions, dividing by a number is the same as multiplying by the reciprocal of that number, so that $\frac{3}{4} \div 2 = \frac{3}{4} \times \frac{1}{2}$.

- 33 -

Multiply the numerators together to obtain the numerator of the product, and multiply the denominators to get the denominator of the product: $\frac{3}{4} \times \frac{1}{2} = \frac{3}{8}$. This division problem can be represented by the diagram shown.

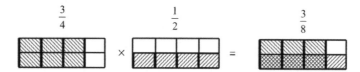

In the first part of the diagram, $\frac{3}{4}$ of the squares are shaded. In the second diagram, $\frac{1}{2}$ of the squares are shaded. Any squares that are shaded in both diagrams will be the answer. The overlap of the two diagrams shows that 3 of the 8 squares overlap, or $\frac{3}{8}$ of the whole. Or, consider dividing the first diagram, which has 6 out of the 8 squares shaded, by two. This would mean taking away half of the shaded squares, which would also result in 3 of the 8 squares shaded, or an answer of $\frac{3}{8}$.

Example problem 2

Ms. Redding is going to frame two new rectangular posters she bought while on vacation. Before placing the order for the frames she needs to know the dimensions of each poster. When she bought the posters she was told that the area of each is $^2/_3$ square yards, the width of one is $^3/_4$ yards and the width of the other is $^1/_2$ yard. Find the length of each poster.

The lengths of the two posters are $^8/_9$ yards and $1\,^1/_3$ yards, respectively. Because $Area = length \times width$ for any rectangle, then $l = \frac{A}{w}$. To solve for the length of each rectangle, divide the area ($^2/_3$ square yards) by each width. When dividing by a fraction you must multiply by the reciprocal of that fraction.

For the first poster, $l = \frac{2}{3} \div \frac{3}{4} = \frac{2}{3} \times \frac{4}{3} = \frac{8}{9}$, and the length of the first poster is $^8/_9$ yards. For the second poster, $l = \frac{2}{3} \div \frac{1}{2} = \frac{2}{3} \times \frac{2}{1} = \frac{4}{3} = 1\,^1/_3$, and the length of the second poster is $1\,^1/_3$ yards.

Expressions

Example problem 1

Simplify the following expressions:

$$(x + 2) \times (x + 2) \times (x + 2)$$
$$(3 - y) \times (3 - y) \times (4x) \times (4x) \times (4x)$$
$$(5 - m) \times (5 - m)^2 \times (6 - m)$$

$(x + 2) \times (x + 2) \times (x + 2) = (x + 2)^3$ This is because there are three instances of $(x + 2)$ being multiplied together, which is the same as raising the quantity $(x + 2)$ to the third power.

$(3 - y) \times (3 - y) \times (4x) \times (4x) \times (4x) = (3 - y)^2 \times (4x)^3$ This is because there are two instances of $(3 - y)$ being multiplied together, which is the same as raising the entity $(3 - y)$ to the second power. That is then being multiplied by three instances of $(4x)$, which is the same as multiplying by $(4x)$ raised to the third power.

$(5 - m) \times (5 - m)^2 \times (6 - m) = (5 - m)^3 \times (6 - m)$ This is because there are three instances of $(5 - m)$ being multiplied together, because $(5 - m)^2 = (5 - m) \times (5 - m)$.

Example problem 2

Evaluate the following:

$$(3 - 1) + 4^2 \times 2$$
$$3^3 + (3 \times 3)$$
$$5^2 - (6 - 2)^2$$

Evaluate these expressions following the order of operations: parentheses, exponents, multiplication/division, and addition/subtraction.

$(3 - 1) + 4^2 \times 2$ is equivalent to 34: $(3 - 1) + 4^2 \times 2 = (2) + 4^2 \times 2 = (2) + 16 \times 2 = (2) + 32 = 34$

$3^3 + (3 \times 3)$ is equivalent to 36: $3^3 + (3 \times 3) = 3^3 + 9 = 27 + 9 = 36$

$5^2 - (6 - 2)^2$ is equivalent to 9: $5^2 - (6 - 2)^2 = 5^2 - (4)^2 = 25 - 16 = 9$

Example problem 3

Simplify the following expressions and identify the terms, products, factors, sums, quotients, and/or coefficients in each:

A. $4x + 3x - 2y$
B. $10(3 + 1)$
C. $\frac{10+5+1}{2}$

There are three terms in the original expression, $4x, 3x,$ and $- 2y$. There are also three coefficients in the expression, $4, 3,$ and $- 2$, respectively. Since $7x$ is the sum of $4x$ and $3x$, the expression simplifies to $7x - 2y$.

There are two terms in the original expression, 3 and 1, and one coefficient, 10, multiplying the sum of the two terms. The sum of 3 and 1 is 4, and the product of 10 and 4 is 40. Therefore, 10 and 4 are factors of 40.

Since we can write this as $(10 + 5 + 1) \div 2$, there are four terms in the original expression, $10, 5, 1$ and 2. The sum of $10, 5,$ and 1 is 16, and the quotient of 16 and 2 is 8. Therefore, 2 and 8 are factors of 16.

Example problem 4

Write expressions to represent the following situations:

Turner has saved $75 toward the purchase of an iPod. How much more money does he need to save?

This week Marcus mowed twice the amount of lawns he mowed last week. How many lawns did Marcus mow this week?

Jenny earns $4 for every room she cleans in her house. How much money will she earn cleaning her whole house?

> Turner has saved $75 toward the purchase of an iPod. The amount of money he still needs to save can be expressed by $C - 75$, representing the difference between total cost, C, of the iPod and what he already has.
>
> This week Marcus mowed twice the amount of lawns he mowed last week. The number of lawns he mowed this week can be expressed as $2l$, representing two times the number of lawns mowed last week, l.
>
> Jenny earns $4 for every room she cleans in her house. The amount of money she will earn cleaning her whole house can be expressed by $4r$, representing 4 times the number of rooms, r, in her whole house.

Example problem 5

Write expressions to represent the following situations and then solve them:

Caroline has 3 more hours of homework tonight than last night. How much homework does Caroline have tonight if she had one hour of homework last night?

This month Fred will only work one-third of the hours he worked last month. How many hours will Fred work this month if he worked 150 hours last month?

> The first part of this situation can be expressed by $h + 3$, representing the number of hours of homework Caroline has tonight in terms of 3 more than she had last night, h. If she had one hour of homework last night, then she has 4 hours of homework tonight, because $1 + 3 = 4$.
>
> This can be expressed by $\frac{w}{3}$, representing the number of hours Fred will work this month in terms of one third of the number he worked last month, w. If he worked 150 hours last month, then he will work 50 hours this month, because $\frac{150}{3} = 50$.

- 36 -

Writing equations

Example problem 1

Write and solve equations that represent the following situations:

You are 16 years old and twice as old as your sister. How old is your sister?

Your mother is 5 times as old as your sister. How old is your mother?

Your cousin's age is the sum of your age and your sister's age. How old is your cousin?

This situation is represented by the equation $2x = 16$, where x represents your sister's age. Solve this equation by dividing both sides by 2, resulting in $x = 8$. Therefore, your sister is 8 years old.

Before we knew your sister's age, this was represented by $m = 5x$, where m is your mother's age and x is your sister's. Since it is now known that your sister is 8 years old, this situation is represented by the equation $5 \times 8 = m$. Solving this equation gives an answer of $5 \times 8 = 40$, so your mother is 40 years old.

Until we knew your sister's age, this was represented by $c = 16 + x$. Since your sister is 8 years, this situation can be represented by the equation $16 + 8 = c$, where c represents your cousin's age. Solving this equation gives an answer of $16 + 8 = 24$, so your cousin is 24 years old.

Example problem 2

Determine the equation that represents the cost, C, for any number of shirts, x, using the table of information below, and find how much it will cost to buy 12 shirts:

Number of Shirts	Cost (in dollars)
1	5
2	10
3	15
4	20

The equation that represents the situation is $C = 5x$. This is found by determining the relationship between the independent variable, which is the number of t-shirts, and the dependent variable, which is the cost. In the table it can be seen that for each shirt bought, the cost goes up by 5 dollars. It is then also seen that multiplying the number of shirts by 5 gives the cost, because $1 \times 5 = 5, 2 \times 5 = 10, 3 \times 5 = 15$, and $4 \times 5 = 20$. Therefore, for any x number of shirts, that number can just be multiplied by 5 to get the cost, which is represented by $C = 5x$.

It will cost $60 to buy 12 shirts. This is found by using the equation that represents the data, substituting 12 for x, the number of shirts: $C = 5 \times 12 = 60$.

Example problem 3

Write the equation to represent the following table of values and graph them. Using the graph, predict the cost of mailing a 6 pound package.

The cost of mailing a package at the post office.

- 37 -

Weight (in lbs)	Cost (in dollars)
1	1.5
2	3
3	4.5
4	6

The equation that represents the cost, C, in terms of the weight, w, of a package is $C = 1.5w$, because for each additional pound, the cost increases by $1.50 per pound. These values are graphed in the graph below:

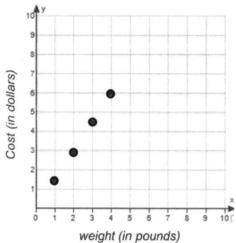

Looking at the graph, the points are going up at a constant rate of $1.50 for each pound. The next point would be at (5, 7.5), and then the next point would be at (6, 9). This means that the cost of mailing a 6 pound package would be $9.

Checking equations

Example problem 1

Match each expression in Column I with its equivalent expression in Column II. Verify that the expressions are equivalent by substituting any non-zero value for x.

Column I
A. $4x$
B. $10x + 12$
C. x

Column II
X. $x + 2x + x$
Y. $3x - x - x$
Z. $3x + 5 + 7x + 7$

A is equivalent to X. If $x = 3$, we see that $4x = 4 \times 3 = 12$, and $x + 2x + x = 3 + 2 \times 3 + 3 = 3 + 6 + 3 = 12$. Since the expressions have the same value when $x = 3$, the expressions are equivalent.

B is equivalent to Z. If $x = 2$, we see that B $= 10x + 12 = 10 \times 2 + 12 = 20 + 12 = 32$, and Z $= 3x + 5 + 7x + 7 = 3 \times 2 + 5 + 7 \times 2 + 7 = 6 + 5 + 14 + 7 = 32$. Since the expressions have the same value when $x = 2$, the expressions are equivalent.

C is equivalent to Y. If $x = 5$, we see that $x = 5$, and $3x - x - x = 3 \times 5 - 5 - 5 = 15 - 5 - 5 = 10 - 5 = 5$. Since the expressions have the same value when $x = 5$, the expressions are equivalent.

Example problem 2

The equation $y = 2x + 5$ represents the line that contains all points (x, y) that satisfy the equation. Decide which, if any, of the following points lie on the line.

$$(1,8) \qquad (0,5) \qquad (2,9) \qquad (2,5)$$

The points $(0,5)$ *and* $(2,9)$ lie on the line. Any points that lie on the line have x and y values that make the equation true. Plug in the first value of each pair for x and the second value of each pair for y, and see whether the equation is true. For the point $(0,5)$: $5 = 2 \times 0 + 5 = 0 + 5 = 5$, and the equation is still true. For the point $(2,9)$: $9 = 2 \times 2 + 5 = 4 + 5 = 9$, and the equation is still true. These points make the equation true and lie on the line. The other two points do not work in the equation. For $(1,8)$: $8 = 2 \times 1 + 5 = 2 + 5 \neq 7$. For $(2,5)$: $5 = 2 \times 2 + 5 = 4 + 5 \neq 9$. (This could also be discovered by referring back to the point $(2,9)$ that is on the line. Since y equals 9 when x is 2, the point $(2,5)$ could be eliminated without testing it in the equation.)

Example problem 3

Solve the inequality for a and check the answer by plugging in a possible value.

$$2a + 6 > 30$$

The solution is $a > 12$. This means that a can be any value greater than 12. This is solved the same way an equation is solved, doing whatever is done to one side of the inequality to the other:

$2a + 6 > 30$ (first subtract 6 from both sides)
$2a > 24$ (divide both sides by 2)

$$a > 12$$

To check the solution, any value that is greater than 12 can be chosen for a. If 20 is chosen, check to see that the left side of the inequality will have a greater value than 30:

$$2 \times 20 + 6 > 30$$
$$40 + 6 > 30$$
$$46 > 30$$

Because it is true that 46 is greater than 30, the inequality was solved correctly.

Example problem 4

Find the solution to the following equation and check the solution by plugging it back into the equation:
$$2p - 11 = 19$$

The solution is $p = 15$. This is found by manipulating the equation to get p by itself on one side of the equal sign. This can be done best by getting rid of the numbers in the reverse order of the normal order of operations. Surrounding the p there is a 2 being multiplied to it and an 11 being subtracted from it. In order of operations, multiplication would be done first and subtraction after, so to undo this expression the subtraction must be handled first, then the multiplication:

$2p - 11 = 19$ (first add 11 to both sides to undo the subtraction by 11)

$2p = 30$ (then divide both sides by 2 to undo the multiplication by 2)

$p = 15$

By plugging the solution back into the original equation it can be verified: $2 \times 15 - 11 = 30 - 11 = 19 = 19$. Since both sides of the equation have a value of 19, the solution is correct.

- 40 -

Table representing an equation

<u>Example</u>

The equation $T = 1l$, represents T, the total time in minutes a racecar driver drives for l number of laps. Determine what the 1 in the equation means, and make a table of values that represents this equation and graph them.

The 1 in the equation represents the time the driver takes to complete one lap. This means that every lap takes the driver 1 minute. The table and graph below show this data:

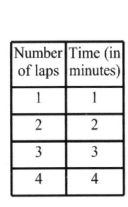

Number of laps	Time (in minutes)
1	1
2	2
3	3
4	4

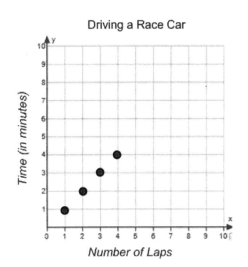

Surface area and volume

<u>Example problem 1</u>

Find the Surface Area and Volume of a cube with side of length 3cm given the following formulas:
$$SA = 6s^2 \text{ and } V = s^3$$

The Surface Area of the cube is 54 square cm and the Volume of the cube is 27 cubic cm. In a cube, the length, width, and height are all the same measurement, which is why the formulas only have one variable, s, which refers to the length of each side. The answers are found by substituting 3 for s in each formula. Surface Area: $SA = 6 \times 3^2 = 6 \times 9 = 54cm^2$. Volume: $V = 3^3 = 27cm^3$.

<u>Example problem 2</u>

Find the Surface Area and Volume of a cylinder with a height of 4cm and radius of 6cm, given the formulas below.

$$SA = 2\pi r^2 + 2\pi rh \text{ and } V = \pi r^2 h$$

The Surface Area of the cylinder is 120π square cm and the Volume of the cylinder is 144π cubic cm. Substitute 4 for h in each formula, since h represents the height, and 6 for r in each formula, since r represents the radius. Surface Area:

$$SA = 2\pi \times 6^2 + 2\pi \times 6 \times 4 = 2\pi \times 36 + 2\pi \times 24 = 72\pi + 48\pi = 120\pi \ cm^2.$$

Volume: $V = \pi \times 6^2 \times 4 = \pi \times 36 \times 4 = 144\pi \ cm^3.$

Area

<u>Example problem 1</u>

Find the area of the following isosceles trapezoid:

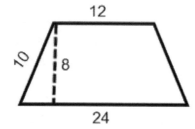

The area of the trapezoid is 144 square units and can be found by breaking the shape into two triangles and one rectangle, like so:

- Since the top base of the trapezoid has a length of 12 and is also the top of the rectangle, then the bottom of the rectangle also has a length of 12. Because the whole base had a length of 24, this leaves 12 for the two bases of the triangles. Dividing this remaining portion in half (because we are told the trapezoid is isosceles) gives each triangle a base of 6. The area of the rectangle is $12 \times 8 = 96$, and the area of each triangle is $\frac{6 \times 8}{2} = \frac{48}{2} = 24$. The total area is then $96 + 24 + 24 = 144$ square units.

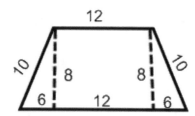

<u>Example problem 2</u>

Mr. Byron is going to buy a new plot of land to build a cabin. The two plots of land are each triangles, but one is a right triangle and the other is an isosceles triangle. Decide which plot will give Mr. Byron the most land to build his cabin using the dimensions given below in feet:

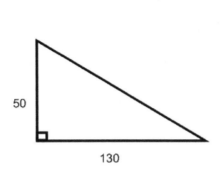
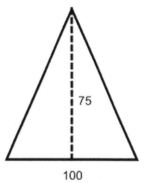

The isosceles triangle will give Mr. Byron the most land, because it has an area of 3750 square feet, while the right triangle only has an area of 3250 square feet. This is found by using the formula for the area of a triangle, $A = \frac{b \times h}{2}$. For the isosceles triangle, $A = \frac{100 \times 75}{2} = \frac{7500}{2} = 3750$ square feet, and for the right triangle, $A = \frac{130 \times 50}{2} = \frac{6500}{2} = 3250$ square feet. Therefore, the plot of land that is an isosceles triangle has an area that is 500 square feet larger than the right triangle, so Mr. Byron will want to purchase that plot.

<u>Example problem 3</u>

Jeremy is staining the cement floor in his basement. He wants to stain the shape of a hexagon in the middle of the floor. He outlines a regular hexagon that has a side of length 6 feet on all sides and a height of 10.4 feet. Find the area Jeremy needs enough stain to cover.

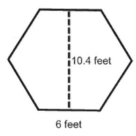

Jeremy will need enough stain to cover 93.6 square feet. This area of the hexagon is found by breaking the hexagon into 6 triangles. Because it is a regular hexagon, each side length is 6 and the height of one triangle is half the height of the whole hexagon, or $\frac{10.4}{2} = 5.2$. Therefore all the triangles are congruent as seen in the diagram below:

- 43 -

Using the formula for area of a triangle, $A = \frac{b \times h}{2}$, each triangle has an area of $\frac{6 \times 5.2}{2} = \frac{31.2}{2} =$ 15.6 square feet. Since each of the 6 triangles has the same area, the total area of the hexagon is then $15.6 \times 6 = 93.6$ square feet.

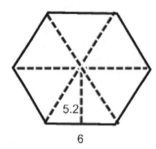

6

Example problem 4

Find the area of the right triangle that has its longest side connecting points A (3, 8) and B (9, 4), and has one horizontal leg and one vertical leg.

The area of this triangle is 12 square units.

To solve for the area, it may be helpful to draw a diagram. Since we are told one leg is horizontal and the other vertical, the legs of the right triangle meet at the ordered pair (3, 4) (or at (9, 8) which would give the same area). The height of the triangle is the distance from (3, 4) to point A at (3, 8) which is 4 units. The base of the triangle is the distance from (3, 4) to point B at (9, 4) which is 6 units. The area of a triangle is found by the formula $A = \frac{b \times h}{2}$ and for this triangle the area is $A = \frac{6 \times 4}{2} = \frac{24}{2} = 12$ units^2.

Volume

Example Problem 1

Ryland Raisin Company is creating new mini-boxes of raisins to sell at school lunches. They have decided to package them in a box that is a cube with dimensions of $\frac{4}{3}$ in $\times \frac{4}{3}$ in $\times \frac{4}{3}$ in.

Find how many mini-boxes with side lengths of $\frac{1}{3}$ in can fit into a raisin box package and what volume the larger box can hold.

There are 64 cubes with side lengths of $\frac{1}{3}$ in that can fit into this new raisin box. The volume of the box is $\frac{64}{27}$ in$^3 = 2\frac{10}{27}$ in^3.

The number of $\frac{1}{3}$ in sided cubes that fit into the box can be found by creating a diagram of the box with its dimensions broken down into $\frac{1}{3}$ in portions as seen below:

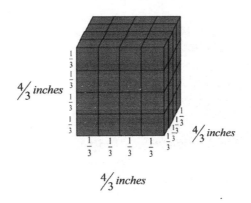

The top row of the box shows there are 16 cubes with sides of $\frac{1}{3}$ in. There are 4 of these rows, which makes a total of $16 \times 4 = 64$ cubes. Since the volume of each little cube is $\frac{1}{3} \times \frac{1}{3} \times \frac{1}{3} = \frac{1}{27}$ in^3, then the total volume is $64 \times \frac{1}{27} = \frac{64}{27} = 2\frac{10}{27}$ in^3. This total volume can also be found by multiplying the dimensions of the raisin box package directly: $\frac{4}{3} \times \frac{4}{3} \times \frac{4}{3} = \frac{64}{27} = 2\frac{10}{27}$ in^3.

Example problem 2

At the grocery store you see two different kinds of cereal on sale for the same price. Box A has dimensions $\frac{3}{4}$ft $\times \frac{1}{2}$ft $\times \frac{2}{3}$ft and Box B has dimensions $\frac{9}{10}$ft $\times \frac{1}{3}$ft $\times \frac{4}{5}$ft. Decide which box will give you the most cereal for your money.

Box A will give you more cereal for your money because the box can hold more volume than Box B. Find the volume of each box using the formula $V = l \times w \times h$. The volume of Box A is $\frac{3}{4} \times \frac{1}{2} \times \frac{2}{3} = \frac{6}{24} = \frac{1}{4}$ ft^3, and the volume of Box B is $\frac{9}{10} \times \frac{1}{3} \times \frac{4}{5} = \frac{36}{150} = \frac{6}{25}$ ft^3. Because $\frac{1}{4} = .25$ and $\frac{6}{25} = .24$, the volume of Box A is slightly larger than the volume of Box B and therefore a better deal because it will hold more cereal.

Mean, median, and mode

Example problem 1

Define the following terms and find each for the data listed below:
- Mean
- Median
- Mode

- 45 -

22, 17, 14, 15, 11, 20, 16, 15, 12, 14, 14

The *Mean* is the average of a set of data. This is found by dividing the sum of the data values by the number of values there are. The mean of the given data is 15.455, which is found by dividing the sum of the data by 11 because there are 11 terms in the data: $\frac{22+17+14+15+11+20+16+15+12+14+14}{11} = 15.455$.

The *Median* is the middle number in a set of data, and can be found by listing the data in order from least to greatest and crossing one off on either end until the middle is reached. If there are two middle terms the average of them is the median of the data. The median of the given data is 15: $11, 12, 14, 14, 14, 15, 15, 16, 17, 20, 22$.

The *mode* is the value in a set of data that occurs the most often. In the given data the mode is 14, because that value occurs 3 times while all other values are only in the list 1 or 2 times.

Example problem 2

The following are the test scores Michaela earned in math class. Her teacher is deciding whether the mean or the median score would best represent Michaela's final grade in math. Based on the data, determine if the teacher should use the mean or the median.

Michaela's Test Scores

50, 55, 58, 58, 90, 92, 99

Michaela's teacher should use the mean test score. The mean test score is found by dividing the sum of the data values by how many there are. The mean of Michaela's test scores is $\frac{50+55+58+58+90+92+99}{7} = \frac{502}{7} = 71.7$. The median of Michaela's test scores is the number in the middle, which is 58: $50, 55, 58, 58, 90, 92, 99$. Since Michaela appears to have improved, it is more reasonable for her to have a passing grade of 71.7% than a failing grade at 58%. Therefore the mean better represents this data.

Example problem 3

You want to go to the ballpark to buy tickets to a baseball game. To ensure that you are able to get tickets you will need to get in the line that has the least waiting time. At the ballpark there are two lines: Red and Blue. You surveyed your friends who have bought tickets in the past to find their wait times. Analyze the data you collected below, decide which line you should wait in to purchase tickets. Time (in minutes):

Red Line: 5, 12, 7, 15, 11, 12, 6, 10, 9 Blue Line: 9, 9, 26, 6, 10, 8, 11, 10, 8

You should wait in the Blue Line. This is because the Red Line has a median wait time of 10 minutes while the Blue Line has a median wait time of 9 minutes. This is found by first listing the data points in order from least to greatest and finding the middle number, which is the median of the data. Crossing off the numbers on the left and right side until reaching the middle will find the middle number: Red Line: $5, 6, 7, 9, 10, 11, 12, 12, 15$ and Blue Line: $6, 8, 8, 9, 9, 10, 10, 11, 26$.

Example problem 4

You have gathered data on the wait times for two different lines at the ballpark. You decide to wait in the Blue Line because it has the lower median wait time. Your friend tells you, however, that you should wait in the Red Line because it has the shortest wait time recorded. Consider the data below, decide if you should change your mind and take your friend's advice.

Time (in minutes):

Red Line: 5, 12, 7, 15, 11, 12, 6, 10, 9 Blue Line: 9, 9, 26, 6, 10, 8, 11, 10, 8

You should not take your friend's advice. You should still choose the Blue Line because the Blue Line's median is 9 minutes, while the Red Line's median is 10 minutes. The data point of 26 in the Blue Line is considered an outlier because it varies greatly from the median compared to the other data points in the set. If you ignore that outlier, the median is still 9! Even ignoring the highest wait time for each line, the mean wait time is higher for the red line, so although the Red Line had the shortest wait time and Blue Line had the longest wait time that is not the best judge of predicting wait time.

Example problem 5

Predict what the median of the data is by analyzing the dot plot below. Calculate the median to check the prediction.

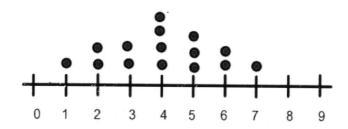

It appears that the median of the data is 4, as its values fall in the middle of all of the dots on the dot plot. Calculating the median is done by first listing the data in order from least to greatest. Each dot on the dot plot represents the number it is above, so therefore the data values are 1, 2, 2, 3, 3, 4, 4, 4, 4, 5, 5, 5, 6, 6, 7. To find the median the values must be

- 47 -

crossed off until the middle number is reached: 1, 2, 2, 3, 3, 4, 4, 4, 4, 5, 5, 5, 6, 6, 7. The appearance of the median in the dot plot is accurate, as the median is 4.

Statistical questions and variability

<u>Example problem</u>

Determine whether the following questions are considered statistical questions and explain why or why not:

'How many pets do the families in my neighborhood have?'

'What size are my shoes?'

'How many pages did I read in the last hour?'

'How long did it take the students in my class to get to school today?'

> Yes, this is a statistical question because it will have variability. The families in your neighborhood will not each have the same number of pets, but there will be a variation in the data collected and conclusions can be drawn from this.

> No, this is not a statistical question. There will be no variation because there is one answer.

> No, this is not a statistical question. There will be no variation because there is one answer.

> Yes, this is a statistical question because it has variability. There will be many different answers to this question and conclusions can be drawn from the data.

Data representation and analysis

<u>Example problem 1</u>

Represent the following data in a dot plot and find the mode of the data:

The amount of money your friends make babysitting per hour

$$5, 2, 7, 9, 4, 5, 6, 7, 9, 7$$

The data is represented in a dot plot below:

The amount of money your friends make babysitting per hour

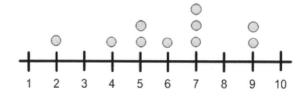

> This is made by creating a number line that can display the range of data and then placing one dot above each number for each data value equal to that number. The mode of this data is 7, which is the number that occurs in the data most. The mode is easy to see in a

- 48 -

dot plot because it is the number that has the most dots. In this data, three people get $7/hour babysitting while only one or two people get paid the other amounts in the list.

Example problem 2

Represent the following data in a box plot:

Michael's math test grades last semester

$$88, 90, 95, 82, 98, 90, 77, 89, 91$$

The data is represented in the box plot below:

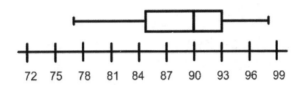

Michael's math test grades last semester

This is made by creating a number line that will fit the distribution of the data and then determining the five points that are needed to create the box plot, which are: the minimum, the maximum, the median, the lower quartile, and the upper quartile. The minimum is the number in the list with the least value, 77, and the maximum is the number with the greatest value, 98. A small tick mark is placed above those two values on the number line. The median of the data is 90, which is found by listing the data in order from least to greatest and finding the number in the middle: 77, 82, 88, 89, 90, 90, 91, 95, 98. The lower quartile is the median of the lower half of the data, which is 85 because the middle of the lower half of the data is between the two middle numbers 82 and 88, and is therefore found by finding their average: $\frac{82+88}{2} = 85.$ The upper-quartile is the median of the upper half of the data, which is 93 because it is between 91 and 95, and their average is $\frac{91+95}{2} = 93.$ A tick mark is placed above the median and upper and lower quartile values on the number line and a box is created around those three marks. A line is then extended from the ends of the box to the minimum and maximum.

Example problem 3

Represent the data below in a histogram:

The amount of homework your friends did last night, in minutes

$$45, 25, 33, 65, 37, 55, 45, 42, 31, 49, 48, 22$$

The histogram below represents the data:

- 49 -

The amount of homework your friends did last night

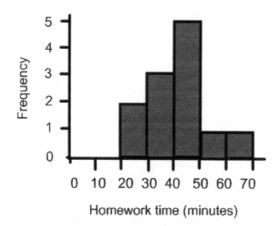

This is made by creating a graph and labeling the *x*-axis with homework time, the *y*-axis with frequency, and creating appropriate intervals for each. (Generally, divide the range of the data into 5 – 7 intervals.) The data values in each interval, which are 10 minute intervals in this histogram, are counted to determine the frequency of data values in those intervals. Adjacent rectangles are created to show the distribution of data. There are 2 pieces of data that fall between 20 and 30 minutes, so that interval has a frequency of 2. There are 3 pieces of data that fall between 30 and 40 minutes, so that interval has a frequency of 3. There are 5 pieces of data that fall between 40 and 50 minutes, so that interval has a frequency of 5. And there is 1 piece of data each that falls between 50 and 60 minutes and 60 and 70 minutes, so those each have a frequency of one.

Example problem 4

Mr. Smith was deciding which of two intersections to post signs at for his garage sale. He sat at one intersection each day for 30 minute time intervals for two consecutive days. Summarize the meaning of his data recorded below and predict what conclusions he may draw.

Number of cars that drove by

Time	Intersection 1	Intersection 2
7am-7:30	8	1
9am-9:30	10	6
11am-11:30	11	10
1pm-1:30	0	9
3pm-3:30	5	10
5pm-5:30	2	4

- 50 -

Mr. Smith will most likely want to place signs for his garage sale at Intersection 2. This is because over the course of the day that Mr. Smith observed Intersection 2, 40 cars drove by, whereas over the course of the day that he observed Intersection 1, only 36 cars drove by. However, Mr. Smith's data shows observations that might make him choose Intersection 1. For example, Mr. Smith might know that morning hours are usually the busiest for garage sales and thus he might want to put his signs at Intersection 1 because more cars drive through that intersection in the morning hours. But, it seems as though the traffic at Intersection 1 tapers off greatly in the afternoon and Mr. Smith might be more concerned with having the possibility of a steady flow of customers at his garage sale all day.

Example problem 5

The local hospital recorded the lengths of the babies born yesterday, given below. Analyze the data and determine what units were being used in the measurements. With the conclusion justify any changes you would recommend for the collection of the data.

Lengths of Babies

$$1.5, 1.75, 2, 16, 17.5, 17.5, 18.5, 19, 20, 20, 21, 22$$

It is clear that there are two different units of measurement being used to measure the lengths of babies. All of the data points between 16 and 22 are reasonable if measured in inches. The data points of 1.5, 1.75, and 2 cannot have been measured in inches and were most likely measured in feet. The data points of 1.5, 1.75, and 2 are reasonable if measured in feet, however all the other pieces of data are not reasonable to have been measured in feet. Therefore, the hospital will need to choose one unit of measure when collecting the data on the lengths of the babies born there. One suggestion would be to measure all babies in inches, and thus change the values of 1.5, 1,75, and 2 in the data to 18, 21, and 24.

Example problem 6

Mr. Gordon is Principal at Detroit's largest Middle School and decided to allow students to choose what time they would eat lunch on a given day. To do this he surveyed a group of students and the data is represented in the histogram below. Principal Gordon concluded that he would allow students to eat at their desired lunch time, 11:00-11:30, because the most students wanted to eat during that time. Explain whether or not Principal Gordon's conclusion was justified based on the data in the histogram.

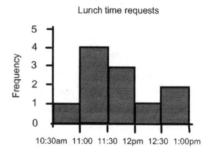

Lunch time requests

No, Mr. Gordon's conclusion is not justified based on the data given in the histogram. Although the majority of the students he surveyed do want to eat lunch between 11 and 11:30, he only surveyed 11 students. This can be found by adding the frequency of each lunch time period. Surveying a group of 11 students might be a reasonable choice for a very small school, but since Mr. Gordon is the Principal at the largest middle school in Detroit, a sample size of 11 students is not enough to draw justifiable conclusions from. It is possible that the majority of all students will want to each lunch between 11 and 11:30, but Mr. Gordon will need a larger sample size to be able to justify the conclusion that it represents the majority of students' preferences.

Net figure

Example problem 1

Sheila is going to make her own canvas tent for camping. She wants to make a tent that is the shape of a triangular prism. Given the dimensions below, create a net figure of the tent and determine how much canvas Sheila will need to make it.

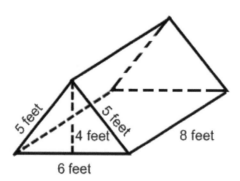

Sheila will need 152 square feet of canvas. This is found by determining the surface area of the triangular prism. In the net figure below, it is clear to see that the sum of the areas of two triangles and three rectangles will give the full surface area.

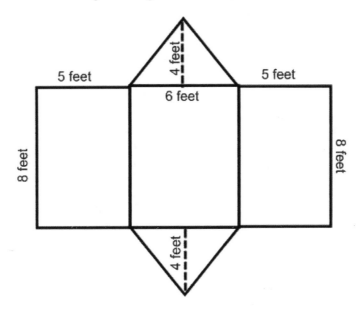

Each triangle has a base of 6 feet and height of 4 feet, so the area of each triangle is $\frac{6 \times 4}{2} = \frac{24}{2} = 12\text{ft}^2$. Each outer rectangle in the net figure has a length of 8 feet and a width of 5 feet, so the area of each of those rectangles is $5 \times 8 = 40\text{ft}^2$. The other rectangle has a length of 8 and a width of 6, so has an area of $6 \times 8 = 48\text{ft}^2$. The total surface area is found by adding the area of all 5 of the separate shapes together: $12 + 12 + 40 + 40 + 48 = 152\text{ft}^2$.

Example problem 2

Draw a net figure of the present below and determine how much wrapping paper will be needed to wrap it.

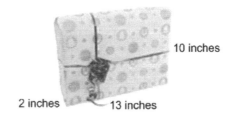

352 square inches of wrapping paper will be needed to wrap the present, which is the surface area of the box. In the net figure below, it is seen that there are two rectangles with dimensions 13in × 2in which each have an area of $13 \times 2 = 26\text{in}^2$, two rectangles with dimensions 10in × 2in which each have an area of $10 \times 2 = 20\text{in}^2$, and two rectangles with dimensions 13in × 10in which each have an area of $13 \times 10 = 130\text{in}^2$. The total

surface area is found by adding together the areas of the 6 rectangles: $26 + 26 + 20 + 20 + 130 + 130 = 352\text{in}^2$.

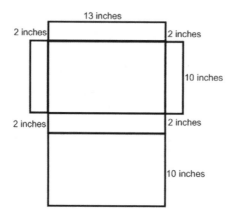

Inequalities

Example problem 1

Write inequalities to represent the following situations, and graph them on number lines:

The speed limit on the highway is 65mph.

Your teacher is older than 30 years old.

    A. This is represented by the inequality $x \leq 65$, because a person can drive at any speed less than or equal to 65mph. This is graphed on the number line below, showing a closed circle on the 65 and an arrow shading to the left, because the safe speeds include 65 and anything less than it:

B. This is represented by the inequality $x > 30$, because your teacher is any age greater than 30 years old, but not equal to 30. This is graphed on the number line below, showing an open circle at 30 and an arrow shading to the right, which means that 30 is not included in the possible ages for your teacher but any number greater is:

25   26   27   28   29   30   31   32   33   34

Example problem 2

Write inequalities to represent the following situations, and give one possible solution for each:

You will not go to school for more than 5 days this week.

Your dad makes at least $100 a day at work.

The bowling alley requires a birthday party size of less than 20 kids.

> This is represented by the inequality $x \leq 5$, because you might go to school 5 days or you might go to school any amount less than that. One solution could be 4, because you might get sick one day this week and only go to school 4 days.

> This is represented by the inequality $x \geq 100$, because your dad will make $100 or more at work each day. One solution could be $125.

> This is represented by the inequality $x < 20$, because there cannot be 20 kids in the party but there can be any amount less than that. One solution could be 15 kids at the birthday party.

Example problem 3

Write an inequality to represent each of the following situations and explain the meaning:

Jim's golf score was 8 under par while Tom's golf score was 2 under par.

> *Water boils at 212°F and freezes at 32°F.*

> *Yesterday the temperature was −17°F and today the temperature is −21°F.*

> If we assume 'par' is like zero on the number line, this can be represented by −8 < −2, which means that it took Tom a greater number of strokes to finish his golf game, because -2 is greater than -8.

> This can be represented by 32° < 212°, which means that the boiling point of water is warmer than the freezing point of water, because 212° is greater than 32°.

> This can be represented by −21° < −17°, which means that it was warmer out yesterday because −17° is greater than −21°.

Example problem 4

Describe scenarios that might correspond to the following inequalities:
$$-20°F < -5°F$$
$$-\$50 < -\$40$$
$$-6 < -2$$

> This represents two different temperatures. One scenario could be that one day it was −20°F in Alaska while the next day it was −5°F there. Since −5°F is greater than −20°F, it was warmer the second day.

> This represents two amounts of money. One scenario could be that Jenny owes the bank $50 while her friend Susan owes the bank $40. Jenny has a greater debt so therefore a more negative balance, and less money than Susan.

> This simply compares two negative integers. One scenario could be that they represent the scores of two golfers. If Max got a golf score of -6 ("six under par") and his friend got a golf score of -2 ("two under par"), then that means it took Max fewer swings to finish the game than it took his friend.

Example problem 5

Represent each scenario below with an absolute value inequality and give one possible solution:
> *A. Last week Mr. Anderson lost 6 of his cattle to Mad Cow Disease and this week he lost even more.*
> *B. Yesterday Andrus took an elevator from his city street underground 4 stories to the subway. Today Andrus took the same elevator down a fewer number of stories.*
> *C. On Monday Sally withdrew $50 from her bank account and on Tuesday she made a larger withdrawal.*

The inequality $|-6| < |x|$ represents the number of cattle Mr. Anderson lost this week, x, compared to the number he lost last week. One possible solution would be $x = -10$, or losing 10 cattle, because $|-6| < |-10|$.

The inequality $|x| < |-4|$ represents how far below ground level Andrus traveled today, x, compared to yesterday. One possible solution would be $x = -1$, or traveling 1 story below ground level, because $|-1| < |-4|$.

The inequality $|-50| < |x|$ represents the amount of Sally's withdrawal on Tuesday, x, compared to her withdrawal Monday. One possible solution would be $x = -100$, or withdrawing $100, because $|-50| < |-100|$.

Example problem 6

Describe a scenario that the following absolute value inequalities could represent:
  A. $|-10 \text{ } feet| > |-3 \text{ } feet|$
  B. $|-300 \text{ } points| > |-50 \text{ } points|$

This inequality could represent the depth of two fish swimming in the ocean. One fish is 10 feet below sea level, or -10 feet, while the other fish is 3 feet below sea level, or -3 feet. The absolute value of -10 is greater than the absolute value of -3, which illustrates the fact the fish swimming 10 feet below sea level is a greater distance from sea level.

This inequality could represent changes in the value of the stock market on two different days. On one day the stock market fell 300 points and the next day the stock market fell 50 points. The absolute value of -300 is greater than the absolute value of -50, illustrating that 300 points is a greater fall than 50 points.

<u>Example problem 7</u>

Write inequalities to represent the following situations, and graph them on number lines:

The minimum cost of a school photo package is $10.

A person has to be less than 48 inches tall to ride the kiddie rides at the amusement park.

This statement is represented by the inequality $x \geq 10$, because you can spend $10 or more on photos. This is graphed on the number line below, showing a closed circle on the 10 and an arrow shading to the right, because the amount you can spend includes 10 dollars or any number greater than that.

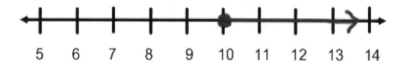

This statement is represented by the inequality $x < 48$ because the acceptable heights are all those less than 48 inches. This is graphed on the number line below, showing an open circle on the 48 and an arrow shading to the left, because 48 is not included in the acceptable heights, but anything less than it is:

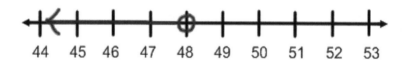

Independent variable and dependent variable

The independent variable is that quantity in a situation that affects the value of the other when changed.

The dependent variable is that quantity in a situation that depends on the value of another variable.

For the following examples:

The total amount of money m you earn for mowing n lawns.

The price p you pay for renting x videos.

The distance d you travel on a bus over time t.

The number of lawns you mow, n, is the independent variable, while the amount of money you earn, m, will depend on how many lawns you mow and thus is the dependent variable.

The number of videos, x, you rent is the independent variable, and the price, p, you pay is the dependent variable because it depends on how many videos you rent.

The time, t, is the independent variable, and the distance, d, is the dependent variable because the distance you travel will depend on how long you travel for.

Opposite

The 'opposite' of a number is the number that is the same distance away from zero as the given number but on the other side of zero on a number line. The 'opposite' of a number always has a sign opposite the given number.

The opposite of -4 is 4.
The opposite of 7 is -7.
The opposite of 21 is -21.
The opposite of -10 is 10.

The opposite of 0 is 0. This is because the only number that is the same distance zero is from zero is zero. Zero is neither positive nor negative, so it will not change signs.

The opposite of 13 is -13.
The opposite of -13 is 13.

Number line

Example problem 1

Label a number line with the following values:

Point A: 2
Point B: The opposite of 3
Point C: 0
Point D: -2
Point E: The opposite of -5
Point F: The opposite of -1

The number line below shows the points:

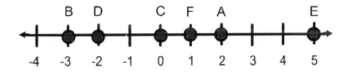

Point A is located at 2 on the number line. Point B is located at -3, which is the opposite of 3. Point C is located at 0. Point D is located at -2. Point E is located at 5, which is the opposite of -5. And Point F is located at 1, which is the opposite of -1.

- 59 -

Example problem 2

Determine the following values, then plot the points on a number line and write an inequality that represents each relation between the points:

5 units to the right of -2

3 units to the left of 1

The number that is 5 units to the right of -2 is 3. The number line below shows these values and it is seen that $3 > -2$ because 3 is located to the right of -2.

The number that is 3 units to the left of 1 is -2. The number line below shows these values and it is seen that $-2 < 1$ because -2 is located to the left of 1.

Example problem 3

Determine the following values, then plot the points on a number line and write an inequality that represents each relation between the points:

1 unit to the left of 1

2 units to the left of -2

A. The number that is 1 unit to the left of 1 is 0. The number line below shows these values and it is seen that $0 < 1$ because 0 is located to the left of 1.

B. The number that is 2 units to the left of -2 is -4. The number line below shows these values and it is seen that $-4 < -2$ because -4 is located to the left of -2.

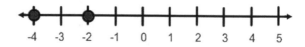

Absolute value

Absolute Value is how far away a number is from zero on a number line, or the distance between zero and that number. The absolute value of a number is always positive, because distance is positive.

The absolute value of 40 is 40, because it is 40 units away from zero.
The absolute value of -12 is 12 because it is 12 units away from zero.

- 60 -

The absolute value of -25 is 25 because it is 25 units away from zero.
The absolute value of 18 is 18 because it is 18 units away from zero.
The absolute value of -100 is 100 because it is 100 units away from zero.

Example problem 1

Write an absolute value equation to express the following situations:

After the first day of a bike race, Peter is 45 seconds behind the lead racer.

Marla owes her mom $10.

The scuba diver is 20 feet below sea level.

> This situation can be represented by $|-45| = 45$. When we say a racer is behind, it actually means that racer's time is longer than the leader's. To catch the leader, then, Peter needs to subtract 45 seconds from his time, and this equation shows that the difference between the times is 45 seconds.

> This situation can be represented by $|-10| = 10$. This shows that Marla is in debt $10 to her mom, but Marla does not actually have a negative amount of money so it is expressed as absolute value, which shows that Marla needs to pay $10 to her mom.

> This situation can be represented by $|-20| = 20$. This shows that the scuba diver is 20 feet under the measurement we mark as '0' on the earth, sea level. However, the scuba diver is not actually a negative distance from sea level so it is expressed in absolute value, showing the scuba diver is a distance of 20 feet away from sea level.

Range

The range helps to quantify the amount of variation in a set of data. It is the difference between the maximum value and the minimum value and can be found by subtracting the minimum value in a set from the maximum value in a set.

Example problem 1

Find the range of each situation below and describe its meaning:

The height of students in Mickey's class (in inches):

58, 62, 59, 61.5, 61, 58, 60, 59.5, 61, 58, 59, 61, 60.5, 58.5

The amount of money each friend spent at dinner (in dollars):

15, 7, 11.50, 21, 14, 17.50, 10, 9, 23.50, 14

For the height of students in Mickey's class the range is 4 inches. The maximum height is 62 inches and the minimum height is 58 inches, so therefore the range is $62 - 58 = 4$. This means that all students in Mickey's class are fairly close together in height as this is a small range to hold all of the data. If the whole class was lined up the difference in height from the tallest person to the shortest would be only 4 inches.

For the amount of money each friend spent at dinner, the range is $16.50. The maximum value is $23.50 and the minimum value is $7, so therefore the range is $23.50 - 7 = 16.50$.

This means that the friends spent a wide range at dinner, meaning some friends bought much more expensive meals or more food than some of the others.

Example problem 2

The following data shows the cost of used cars in the sales lot. Plot the data on a line plot and describe the meaning of the range of data.

Price of Used Cars For Sale (in dollars)

14,000	7,500	8,000	600
19,000	18,500	9,500	3,000
5,500	950	16,000	2,000

The data is displayed on the line plot below:

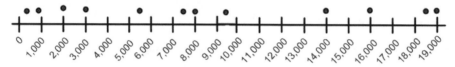

Price of cars (in dollars)

The range of the data is $18,400. This is found by subtracting the smallest value, $600, from the largest value, $19,000. This is a large range for the price of the cars in the lot. Looking at the line plot it is easy to see that the prices of cars are very spread out. This might mean that the lot has some fairly new used cars and also some very old cars for sale.

Example problem 3

The following table shows the amount of television each student watched the night before the math test. Any student who watched television for a greater amount of time than the median earned a D on the test. Find the range of the data and determine who got a D on the test.

Student	Hours of TV watched	Student	Hours of TV watched
Billy	1	Brock	2
Paige	6	Colleen	3.5
Margaret	.5	Courtney	0
Skylar	2	Blair	3
James	0	Theresa	1
Fiona	0	Tyler	4.5
Kyle	3	Troy	1.5

The range of the data is 6 hours. This is found by subtracting the smallest value, 0, from the largest value, 6.

The median of the data must be found in order to determine who earned a D on the test. The median of the data is 1.75 hours. This is found by ordering the numbers from least to greatest and finding the middle number, like so: 0, 0, 0, .5, 1, 1, 1.5, 2, 2, 3, 3, 3.5, 4.5, 6. Since there are two numbers in the middle of the data, the average of those two must be found. Therefore, the median of the data is $\frac{1.5+2}{2} = \frac{3.5}{2} = 1.75$. Since any student who watched TV for more than 1.75 hours earned a D on the test, Paige, Skylar, Kyle, Brock, Colleen, Blair, and Tyler all earned D's on the test.

Example problem 4

The students in Mark's class filled in the table to represent how many siblings they each have. Use the table to find the range of the data and describe the shape made by a line plot of the data.

Number of siblings	Number of students
0	||
1	||||
2	⊞⊞||
3	|||
4	||
5	
6	|

The range of the data is 6. This is found by subtracting the smallest number, 0, from the largest number, 6. The shape of the line plot of this data is similar to a bell curve, or that of a small hill. The majority of the dots are above the 2, which is the mode of the data because it occurs most frequently. It is also the median of the data, because it is the value in the middle. The dots on either side of 2 are similar-sized groups getting smaller the farther away from 2 the values get. This can be seen in the line plot below:

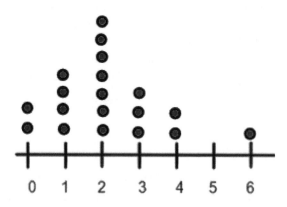

Example problem 5

Given the following graph of data of four students' speeds to walk to school, determine what units must have been used.

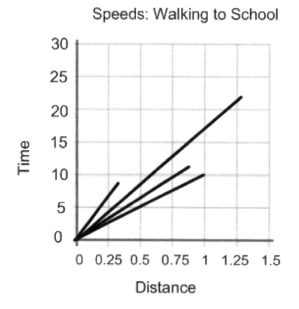

The units that must have been used are Distance in Miles and Time in Minutes. If the distance measurement is considered first, there is no other reasonable measurement other than miles. It would not make sense for the measurements to be in feet, as walking less than 1.5 feet to school would not be considered because everyone has to walk at least a few feet to get into the building, and no one can live 1.5 feet from the school. Similarly, meters or yards or anything less than those would also not be a reasonable measurement.

Considering that the distance is measured in miles, the most likely unit of time measurement is in minutes. Hours is very unreason-able as it would not take someone

- 64 -

over 20 hours to walk 1.25 miles, and seconds is as equally unreasonable as it would not take someone just over 20 seconds to walk 1.25 miles.

The only other possible measurement would be distance in kilometers, but the times in minutes are maybe a little too slow to represent walking distances in kilometers.

Important terms

- *Sample size* — Sample size is the number of people surveyed or the number of observations made in a statistical experiment. For example, if the mayor of a town surveyed 800 residents to determine the town's opinion on a new park, then the sample size is 800 and the mayor has hopefully judged that this will be a large enough sample to represent the whole population.
- *Data set* — Data set is a list, or set, of all the numbers or values that are the results from a statistical experiment. An example would be that the following data set represents the shoe sizes of Fred's friends: {6, 7.5, 8, 8, 8.5, 9.5, 10}. That list of numbers is the data set and each number represents the shoe size of Fred's friends.
- *First quartile* — The first quartile is the number that is the median of the lower half of a data set that is, the half between the minimum and the median. All pieces of data less than the first quartile are in the lowest 25% of the data. It can also be referred to as the 'lower quartile'.
- *Second quartile* — The second quartile is more commonly called the median, and is the middle number of a data set. It splits the data in half, so that 50% of the data is less than this number and 50% of the data is greater than this number.
- *Third quartile* — The third quartile is the number that is the median of the upper half of a data set, that is, the half between the median and the maximum. All pieces of data greater than it are in the top 25% of the data. It can also be referred to as the 'upper quartile'.
- *Maximum* — The maximum is the greatest value in a data set.
- *Minimum* — The minimum is the least value in a data set.
- *Integer* — An integer is any whole number, including 0 and all the negative whole numbers as well. The values $-100, -12, -1, 4,$ and 13 are all integers because they are all whole numbers, whether positive or negative. The values -2.65, $\frac{1}{3}$, and $\sqrt{6}$ are not integers because they are not whole numbers.
- *Rational number* — A rational number is any number that can be expressed as a fraction. Equivalently, a rational number is any number that can be expressed as a terminating or repeating decimal. Rational numbers can be both positive and negative. The values $-\frac{2}{5}$ and 3 are rational numbers because $-\frac{2}{5}$ is a fraction and 3 can be expressed as a fraction as $\frac{3}{1}$. Any integer can be expressed as a fraction as itself over 1, so all integers are also rational numbers. The values $\sqrt{8}$ and π are not rational numbers (they are called 'irrational numbers') because they cannot be expressed as a fraction. These numbers are decimals that continue on without ending or repeating.
- *Prime number* — A prime number is a number that is only evenly divisible by 1 and itself.
- *Prime factor* — A prime factor is a prime number that divides evenly into another number. For example, 3 is a prime factor of 21, because 3 is a prime number and 21 is evenly divisible by 3.
- *Least common multiple* — The least common multiple is the smallest number that is evenly divisible by all numbers in a given set.
- *Greatest common factor* — The greatest common factor is the greatest number that all numbers in a set are evenly divisible by.
- *Quotient* — The result of a division operation. For example, the quotient of 10 and 5 is 2.
- *Product* — The result of a multiplication operation. For example, the product of 6 and 3 is 18.

- *Sum* — The result of an addition operation. For example, the sum of 4 and 7 is 11.
- *Difference* — The result of a subtraction operation. The difference between two numbers can be thought of as the distance between them on a number line. For example, the difference of 12 and 8 is 4.
- *Factor* — A factor is a number divides evenly into a given number. For example, 4 is a factor of 8, because 8 is evenly divisible by 4.
- *Coefficient* — A coefficient is a number that multiplies a variable and that denotes how many instances of that variable are represented together. This number is written in front of, or to the left of, the variable. There is generally no multiplication sign between the coefficient and the variable. For example, in the term '3x', 3 is the coefficient.
- *Term* — A term is a number or variable or a product of number(s) and/or variable(s) that does not contain an operation symbol. For example, in the expression $y + 4x + 7$, y, 4x, and 7 are separate terms.
- *Expression* — An expression is a group of one or more numbers variables, and/or terms that are combined together with operations. There is no equal sign in an expression. For example, $7x - (2x + 3) \div 4$ is an expression.
- *Variable* — A variable is an unknown value represented by a letter in an expression or equation. A variable can represent one value or a set of values. For example, in the equation $2x + 4 = 10$, x is a variable and has one value. In the equation $y = 8x + 1$, x and y can have multiple values as long as they both make the equation true.
- *Equation* — An equation is a relationship equating two expressions. An equation can be distinguished from an expression by the equal sign. For example, $4x = 12$ is an equation because it has an equal sign.
- *Inequality* — An inequality is a comparison between two or more expressions that are not necessarily equal; one might be greater or less than another. Because of this, when solving an inequality for a variable, the solution is a range of values. For example, $5a + 2 \leq 22$ is an inequality because it has a "less than or equal to" symbol between the two expressions.

Practice Test #1

Practice Questions

1. Antonio wants to buy a roll of border to finish an art project. At four different shops, he found four different borders he liked. He wants to use the widest of the borders. The list shows the width, in inches, of the borders he found.

$$1\frac{7}{10}, 1.72, 1\frac{3}{4}, 1.695$$

Which roll of border should Antonio buy if he wants to buy the widest border?

    a. $1\frac{7}{10}$
    b. 1.72
    c. $1\frac{3}{4}$
    d. 1.695

2. Daniella wrote a decimal and a fraction which were equivalent to each other. Which pair of numbers could be the pair Daniella wrote?

    a. $0.625, \frac{7}{8}$
    b. $0.375, \frac{3}{8}$
    c. $0.75, \frac{7}{5}$
    d. $0.45, \frac{4}{5}$

3. Glenda poured salt into three salt shakers from a box that contained 19 ounces of salt. She poured 5 ounces of salt into one shaker. She divided what was left evenly into the other two shakers. Which equation best represents this scenario?

    a. 19-5-2(7)=0
    b. 5+2+7=19
    c. 19-2-7-7=0
    d. 19-2(5)-7=0

4. Large boxes of canned beans hold 24 cans of beans and small boxes hold 12 cans. One afternoon, Gerald brought 4 large boxes of canned beans and 6 small boxes of canned beans to the food bank. How many cans of beans did Gerald bring to the food bank that afternoon?

    a. 168
    b. 192
    c. 288
    d. 360

5. Enrique used a formula to find the total cost, in dollars, for repairs he and his helper, Jenny, made to a furnace. The expression below shows the formula he used, with 4 being the number of hours he worked on the furnace and 2 being the number of hours Jenny worked on the furnace.

$$20 + 35(4 + 2) + 47$$

What is the total cost for repairing the furnace?

    a. $189
    b. $269
    c. $277
    d. $377

6. One morning at Jim's café, 25 people ordered juice, 10 ordered milk, and 50 ordered coffee with breakfast. Which ratio best compares the number of people who ordered milk to the number of people who ordered juice?

    a. 5 to 7
    b. 5 to 2
    c. 2 to 7
    d. 2 to 5

7. Which expression best shows the prime factorization of 750?

    a. $2 \times 3 \times 5^3$
    b. $2 \times 3 \times 5^2$
    c. $2 \times 3 \times 5 \times 25$
    d. $2 \times 3 \times 5^2 \times 25$

8. At the middle school Vanessa attends, there are 240 Grade 6 students, 210 Grade 7 students, and 200 Grade 8 students. Which ratio best compares the number of students in Grade 8 to the number of students in Grade 6 at Vanessa's school? Explain why your answer is correct.

    a. $5 : 6$
    b. $5 : 11$
    c. $6 : 5$
    d. $7 : 8$

_____

_____

_____

9. A display at the bottom of the laptop computer Erica was using showed that the battery had a 70% charge. Which decimal is equivalent to 70%?

    a. 0.07
    b. 70.0
    c. 7.0
    d. 0.7

10. The drawing shows a chart used to record completed Math assignments. A checkmark is used to show which assignments are finished.

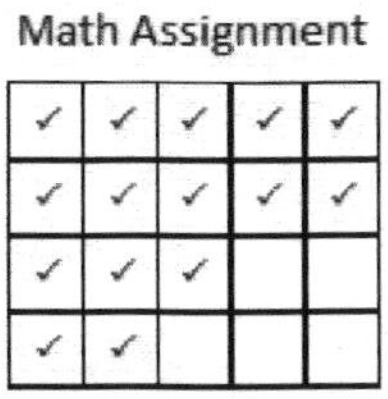

Math Assignment

✓	✓	✓	✓	✓
✓	✓	✓	✓	✓
✓	✓	✓		
✓	✓			

Which of the following shows the percentage of Math assignments in the chart which are finished?
   a. 15%
   b. 25%
   c. 55%
   d. 75%

11. Harold learned that 6 out of 10 students at his school live within two miles of the school. If 240 students attend Grade 6 at his school, about how many of these students should Harold expect to live within two miles of the school?
   a. 24
   b. 40
   c. 144
   d. 180

12. A unit of liquid measure in the English System of Measure is the gill. The table, shown here, gives conversions from gills to fluid ounces.

Conversion Table

Gills	Fluid Ounces
2	8
4	16
5	20
6	24
10	40

Which equation best describes the relationship between gills, g, and fluid ounces, f?
   a. $f = 8g - 8$
   b. $f = 2g + 4$
   c. $f = 4g$
   d. $4f = g$

13. The drawing shows a window with equal-sized panes. Some of the panes are not tinted, some are tinted a light shade of gray, and some are tinted a very dark shade of gray.

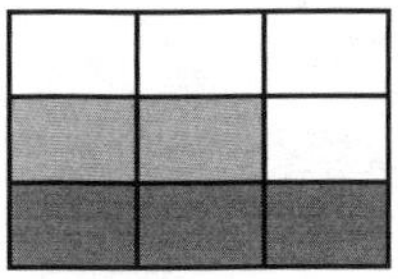

Which number sentence best models the total section of the window that has tinted panes?

a. $\frac{1}{3} + \frac{1}{3} = \frac{2}{3}$

b. $\frac{1}{3} + \frac{2}{9} = \frac{5}{9}$

c. $\frac{1}{9} + \frac{2}{3} = \frac{7}{9}$

d. $\frac{2}{9} + \frac{4}{9} = \frac{2}{3}$

14. The table below shows changes in the area of several trapezoids as the lengths of the bases, b_1 and b_2, remain the same and the height, h, changes.

Trapezoids

b_1 (in feet)	b_2 (in feet)	h (in feet)	A (in square feet)
5	7	2	12
5	7	4	24
5	7	6	36
5	7	8	48

Which formula best represents the relationship between A, the areas of these trapezoids, and h, their heights?

a. $A = 5h$

b. $A = 6h$

c. $A = 7h$

d. $A = 12h$

15. This table shows lengths, widths, and areas of four rectangles. In each rectangle, the length remains 40 meters, but the width changes.

Rectangles

Length	40 meters	40 meters	40 meters	40 meters
Width	20 meters	30 meters	40 meters	50 meters
Perimeter	120 meters	140 meters	160 meters	180 meters

Which formula best represents the relationship between P, the perimeters of these rectangles, and w, their widths? Explain the process you used to find your answer.

a. $P = w + 80$

b. $P = 2w + 80$

c. $P = 2(2w + 40)$

d. $P = 10(w + 40)$

_____

_____

_____

16. Thomas drew a polygon with vertices: A, B, C, and D. He measured the angles formed and recorded the information shown here.

$$m\angle A = 70°, m\angle B = 80°, m\angle C = 120°, m\angle D = 90°$$

- 70 -

Which of the angles that Thomas drew is an obtuse angle?

    a. $\angle A$
    b. $\angle B$
    c. $\angle C$
    d. $\angle D$

17. In $\triangle RST$, shown here, $m\angle S$ is 20° less than $m\angle R$.

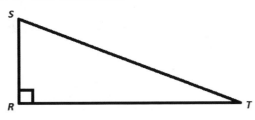

What is the measure of $\angle T$?

    a. 110°
    b. 70°
    c. 50°
    d. 20°

18. A trash company charges a fee of $80 to haul off a load of trash. There is also a charge of $0.05 per mile the load must be hauled. Which equation can be used to find c, the cost for hauling a load of trash m miles?

    a. $80(m + 0.05)$
    b. $0.05(m + 80)$
    c. $80m + 0.05$
    d. $0.05m + 80$

19. Ellen measured $\angle R$ in the parallelogram shown here and found it to be 35°. She knows that $\angle R$ and $\angle T$ have equal measures. She also knows $\angle S$ and $\angle V$ are equal in measure.

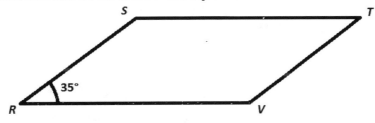

What is the measure of $\angle V$?

    a. 215°
    b. 145°
    c. 70°
    d. 35°

20. Which expressions are equivalent to 4(2n-6)? Select all that apply.

    1. 4n(2-6)
    2. 8n-24
    3. 8n+24

4. 2(2n-6)+2(2n-6)
5. 5(2n-6)-(2n-6)

21. A store buys sodas from the manufacture for $3.60 a case. There are 24 sodas in a case. They sell them for $.35 per soda. How much profit do the make on one soda?

_____

22. Jessica wrote down the times required for five girls to run a race. The times are shown in this list.

25.1 seconds, 24.9 seconds, 25.2 seconds, 24.8 seconds, 25.0 seconds

What time is closest to the total for all five runners?
a. 1 minute and 5 seconds
b. 1 minute and 25 seconds
c. 2 minutes and 5 seconds
d. 2 minutes and 25 seconds

23. This drawing shows an equilateral triangle and a ruler.

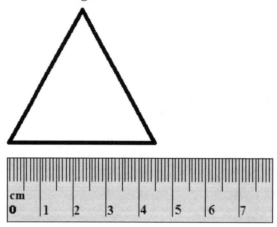

Which is closest to the perimeter of the triangle?
a. 4.5 centimeters
b. 9.0 centimeters
c. 13.5 centimeters
d. 20.3 centimeters

24. The drawing shows a protractor and a trapezoid.

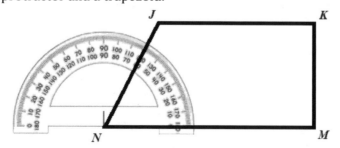

Which is closest to the measure of ∠JNM?

- 72 -

a. 61°
b. 79°
c. 119°
d. 121°

25. Given the equation $a^2 + (2b - c) \times d$, solve for a=2, b=5, c=8, and d=4. Explain the steps you took to solve this problem.

_____

_____

_____

26. Mega Book Store is selling books for 30% off. James wants to buy 3 books. The regular prices of the books are $8, $12, and $15. What is the total price he should expect to pay during the sale?

a. $35
b. $25
c. $24.50
d. $23.50

27. Stephen researched the topic of solar-powered lights for his science project. He exposed 10 new solar lights to five hours of sunlight. He recorded the number of minutes each light continued to shine after dark in the list below.

63, 67, 73, 75, 80, 91, 63, 72, 79, 87

Which of these numbers is the mean of the number of minutes in Stephen's list?

a. 28
b. 63
c. 74
d. 75

28. Grade 6 students at Fairview Middle School were asked to name their favorite of six school subjects. The plot below shows a summary of their answers. Each X represents 5 students.

Favorite School Subject

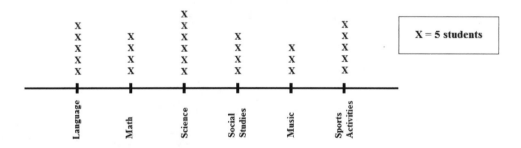

- 73 -

Which graph best represents the data in the plot?

a.

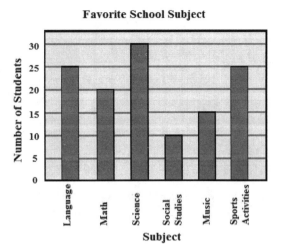

c.

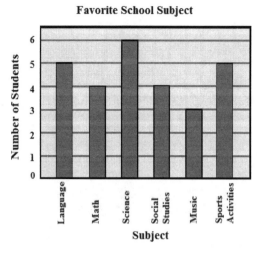

b.

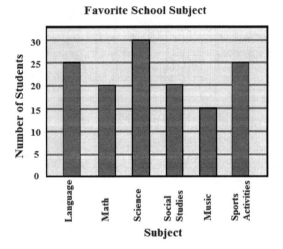

d.

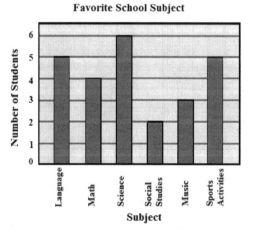

29. Hillside Middle School students are choosing school colors from three dark colors (black, blue, and brown) and two light colors (white and yellow). Which tree diagram best shows all possible color combinations of one dark color and one light color?

a.

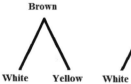

b.

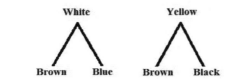

c.

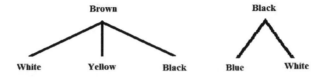

d.

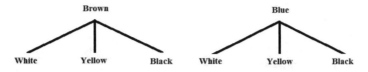

30. Sammie had $120 he had earned doing chores for people in his neighborhood. When school started, he spent $50 for shirts, $30 for jeans, and $40 for school supplies. Which graph best represents how Sammy spent his $120?

a.

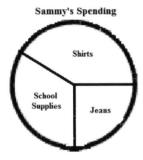

c.

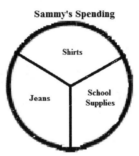

b.

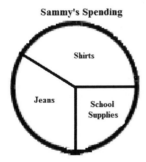

d.

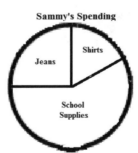

- 75 -

31. James and his driving partner, Larissa, recently drove a truck from Dallas, TX to Los Angeles, CA. The total distance they drove was 1,380 miles. James is paid $0.35 per mile he drives and Larissa is paid $0.30 per mile she drives. What additional information is needed to find the amount James should be paid for the trip?

    a. The total number of hours each person drove
    b. The total number of miles each person drove
    c. The total amount of fuel the truck used
    d. The total weight of the truck and cargo

32. Petra installed 10 light fixtures at a new warehouse that was being built. Each of the fixtures required 3 light bulbs. The bulbs come in packages of 5 and cost $8 per package. What was the total cost for the bulbs required for all of the fixtures Petra installed at the warehouse?

    a. $16
    b. $48
    c. $120
    d. $240

33. Anna and other members of her club sold caps to commemorate their city's 100th birthday. The caps sold for $14 and came in four colors. The club made $3,360 in total sales from selling the caps. The graph below shows the part of the total sales that each color represented.

Colors of Caps Sold

Which number is closest to the combined number of white and pink caps sold by Anna's club members? Explain why your answer is correct.

    a. 40
    b. 80
    c. 120
    d. 160

_____

_____

_____

34. Gabe has 6 pencils. The lengths of his pencils in inches are shown on the number line below. What is the mean length of the pencils? Explain why your answer is correct.

a. 7 in.

b. $7\frac{1}{4}$ in.

c. $7\frac{1}{2}$ in.

d. $6\frac{3}{4}$ in.

_____

_____

_____

35. Jason wants to put dry fertilizer on the grass in his front yard. The yard is 20 feet wide and 45 feet long. Each pound of the fertilizer he plans to use is enough for 150 square feet. Which procedure could Jason use to determine the correct amount of fertilizer to use on the entire yard?

a. Divide 150 by 20 and divide 150 by 45, and then add those quotients together
b. Add 20 and 45, double that total, and then divide that total by 150
c. Multiply 20 by 45, and then subtract 150 from that product
d. Multiply 20 by 45, and then divide that product by 150

36. An electronics store sells laptops for $475. They are on sale for $380. Which equation below represents this? Let *r* represent the regular price of laptops and *s* represent the sale price.

a. $r=.8s$
b. $s=.2r$
c. $s=.7r$
d. $s=.8r$

37. Kerianne collected the weights of her friends. What is the range of her friends' weight?

55 lbs, 63 lbs, 48 lbs, 72 lbs, 61 lbs, 68 lbs

_____

38. What is the greatest common factor of 66 and 24?

_____

39. Point *A* on the graph below is reflected across the x-axis and then translated 3 units left. At what coordinates does it end up?

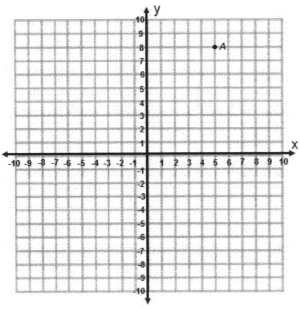

   a. (2,8)
   b. (2, −8)
   c. (−2, 8)
   d. (5, −8)

40. Candace's shoelace broke. She measured the unbroken shoelace and finds that she needs a replacement lace that is at least 16 inches long. The store has the following lengths available.

$$15\frac{7}{10}\ ,16.25\ ,\frac{47}{3}\ ,15.5$$

Which one of the following lace lengths would be long enough to replace the broken shoelace?

   a. $15\frac{7}{10}$
   b. 16.25
   c. $\frac{47}{3}$
   d. 15.5

41. Nadia is working summer jobs. She earns $5 for every dog she walks, $2 for bringing back a trashcan, $1 for checking the mail, and $5 for watering the flowers. Nadia walks 3 dogs, brings back 5 trashcans, checks the mail for 10 neighbors, and waters the flowers at 6 houses. Which expression can be used to find out how much money Nadia earned?

   a. $2(5) +$6(10) + $1
   b. $10(6) + $1 + $5
   c. $5(3+6) + $2(5) + $1(10)
   d. $15 + $10 + $16

- 78 -

42. Only 8% of the dogs were solid white. Which decimal is equivalent to 8%?

    a. 0.08

    b. 80.0

    c. 8.0

    d. 0.8

43. Use this grid to answer the question.

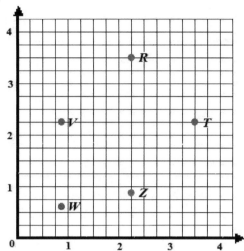

Which of the points on the grid best represents the point at $(2\frac{1}{4}, \frac{7}{8})$?

    a. T

    b. V

    c. W

    d. Z

44. Part A: A restaurant is trying to attract a younger crowd. They think that they have managed to attract more young people but wanted to graph their results to see. The ages of 40 guests are given below. Create a histogram to show the results.

23	26	21	42	35	29	53	31
19	24	27	30	22	37	21	25
22	26	30	34	27	20	50	41
32	23	18	20	39	22	33	35
25	30	27	19	24	42	47	21

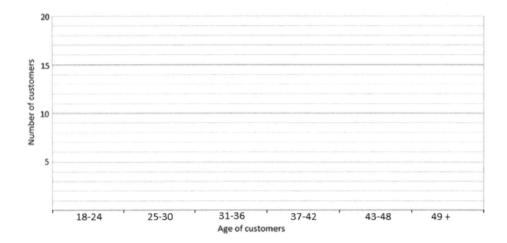

Part B: If they wanted the median age of the customers to be in the 24-30 range were they successful?

_____

45. Zach created a machine that could take a number x and put it into the equation $y = 2x^2 - 3x + 4$, and give an answer y. Use the following numbers to fill in the equation, and make a true statement.

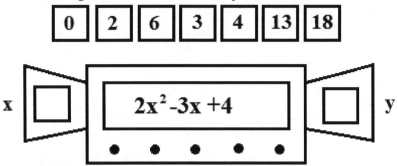

46. Antoinette had $50 she had saved. At a craft show, she bought 2 pairs of earrings for $10 each and a picture for $12. She also spent $7 on lunch. If she spent no other money, how much money should Antoinette have left from the $50?

a. $35, because 50 – (10 +12) + 7 = 35
b. $25, because 50 – [2(10) +12] + 7 = 25
c. $21, because 50 – (10 + 12 + 7) = 21
d. $11, because 50 – [2(10) + 12 +7] = 11

Answers and Explanations

1. C: To answer this question correctly, convert all numbers to decimal form to make them easy to compare. Since two of the numbers are already in decimal form, we only need to convert $1\frac{7}{10}$ and $1\frac{3}{4}$ to decimal form.

$$7 \div 10 = 0.7, \text{ so } 1\frac{7}{10} = 1.7$$
$$\text{and } 3 \div 4 = 0.75, \text{ so } 1\frac{3}{4} = 1.75$$

Therefore, by comparing place values from left to right of 1.7, 1.72, 1.75 and 1.695, we see that 1.695 is least, 1.7 is next greatest, 1.72 is next, and 1.75 is greatest. So, Antonio should buy the border that is $1\frac{3}{4}$ inches wide.

2. B: To answer this question, one method that can be used is to convert all the fractions to decimal form so it is easier to compare them to each other. This can be done by simply dividing, since the fraction sign means division.

$$7 \div 8 = 0.875$$
$$3 \div 8 = 0.375$$
$$7 \div 5 = 1.4$$
$$4 \div 5 = 0.8$$

So, the only pair of numbers in which the fraction is equivalent to the decimal is in answer B.

3. A: She starts with 19 ounces and then subtracts 5. Then she has 14 ounces and divides that by 2 which gives her 7 ounces per shaker. Thus the equation: 19-5-2(7)=0

4. A: Multiply 24 by 4 to get 96 and multiply 12 by 6 to get 72. Then, add 96 and 72 to get the correct answer, 168.

5. C: To solve this formula, follow the order of operations. First, add what is in the parenthesis, 4 + 2, to get 6. Then, multiply the 6 by 35 to get 210. Last, we should add 20 + 210 + 47 to get 277.

6. D: Note that the ratio asked for is the number of people who ordered milk to the number who ordered juice. The number of people who ordered coffee does not matter here. This compares 10 to 25, and the order is important here. Since the ratio is with the number of people who ordered milk first, the 10 must come first. So, the ratio is 10 to 25, but the ratio can be written in simpler form by dividing both numbers in the ratio by 5, to get the ratio: 2 to 5.

7. A: There is more than one way to solve this problem. One method is to use the fact that the number ends in 0. This means 10 is a factor. So, $10 \times 75 = 750$. The factor 10 has prime factors of 2 and 5. The factor 75 has factors of 3 and 25 and the 25 has two factors of 5. Putting the prime factors in order, least to greatest, and showing the three factors of 5 with an exponent of 3 gives us answer A: $2 \times 3 \times 5^3$.

8. A: One way to answer this question is to name the ratio: 200 to 240, then write the ratio in simplest terms by dividing both terms by the greatest common factor, 40, to get 5 to 6. It should be noted that the number of Grade 7 students is not important for this problem. Also, the order of the ratio matters. Since it asks for the ratio using the number of Grade 8 students first, the ratio is 200 to 240 and not the other way around.

9. D: To correctly write a percent as a decimal, the percent sign is dropped and the number is rewritten with the decimal point two places to the left. This is because a percent is always a value out of 100 and the second place after the decimal point is the hundredths place. So, 70% = 0.70 and the zero at the end after the decimal can be dropped.

10. D: There are 15 of the 20 assignments with check marks indicating a finished assignment. Since the fraction $\frac{1}{20}$ represents 5%, then 15 times 5% gives 75% of the assignments finished.

11. C: One way to find this answer is to set up a proportion: $\frac{6}{10} = \frac{G}{240}$, in which G represents the number of Grade 6 students living within two miles of the school. To solve the proportion, we should cross-multiply. So, 10 times G = 6 times 240. This gives the equation:

$10G = 1,440$. To solve the equation we divide both sides of the equation by 10, which gives $G = 144$.

12. C: Looking at the chart, a pattern can be seen in the relationship between the number of gills and the number of fluid ounces. Each number of gills in the first column, when multiplied by 4, gives the number of fluid ounces in the second column. So, f equals 4 times g, or $f = 4g$.

13. B: To answer this question, that there are 9 equal-sized panes in the window. Of the 9 panes, 3 have a dark tint and can be represented by the fraction, $\frac{3}{9}$, which is equivalent to $\frac{1}{3}$. 2 of the panes are lightly tinted and can be represented by $\frac{2}{9}$. So, the number sentence, $\frac{1}{3} + \frac{2}{9} = \frac{5}{9}$ best represents the total section of the window which is tinted.

14. B: The formula for the area of trapezoids is not necessarily needed here to do this problem. Since the relationship between the area, A, and the height, h, can be seen in the chart, looking at the third and fourth columns to see if there is a pattern will show a relationship between the variables. Each value in the area column is equal to 6 times the value in the height column. So, we get $A = 6h$.

15. B: To answer this question, start with the perimeter formula, $P = 2(l + w)$ and substitute values that are known to remain the same. So, $P = 2(l + w)$ becomes $P = 2(40 + w)$. Then we distribute, multiplying both numbers inside the parenthesis by 2 and get $P = 80 + 2w$. Writing the variable first in the expression gives us: $P = 2w + 80$.

16. C: An obtuse angle measures between 90 and 180 degrees and $\angle C$ is the only choice which measured in that range.

17. D: The box symbol shown at $\angle R$ means that $\angle R$ measures 90°. Since we are told $m\angle S$ is 20° less than $m\angle R$, subtract 90 –20 to get 70. This means that $m\angle S = 70°$. The sum of $m\angle R$ and $m\angle S$ is found by adding: 90 +70 = 160. The sum of all angles in a triangle always adds up to 180°, so subtracting 180 – 160 results in a difference of 20. So, $m\angle T$ is 20°.

18. D: The amount charged for miles hauled will require us to multiply the number of miles by $0.05. The charge for each load of $80 is not changed by the number of miles hauled. That will be added to the amount charged for miles hauled. So, the equation needs to show 0.05 times miles plus 80, or $c = 0.05m + 80$.

19. B: The angles opposite each other in a parallelogram are equal in measure. So, $\angle R$ has an equal measure to $\angle T$, or 35°. The sum of the measures of these two angles is 35 + 35 = 70. The sum of the measures of all four angles of a quadrilateral is 360°. We subtract 360 – 70 to get 290. So, 290° is the sum

- 83 -

of the measures of the other two equal angles, $\angle S$ and $\angle V$. Then we divide 290 by 2 to get 145. We know that $\angle V$ has a measure of 145°.

20. II, V: First distribute in the 4 to get $8n - 24$. Then do the same for all of the answer choices and see which ones equal $8n - 24$.

21. $.20: First find what it costs the store per coke. So, divide $3.60 by 24 to get $.15 per soda. Then they sell them for $.35 per soda so they make $.20 per soda.

22. C: A close estimate for the total time for all five runners is 125 seconds, which is found by adding 25.1 + 24.9 + 25.2 + 24.8 + 25.0. Then, to convert seconds to minutes, divide by 60 seconds (since there are 60 seconds in a minute) to get 2 with remainder of 5, or 2 minutes and 5 seconds.

23. C: The ruler is used to determine the length of one side of the triangle, which is about 4.5 centimeters. Since this is an equilateral triangle, all three sides are of equal length. To find the perimeter, we add up all of the sides. However, since they are all the same length, we can just multiply 4.5 centimeters by 3 to get 13.5 centimeters.

24. A: Since segment NM lies along the right side of the protractor, we read the inside scale. The segment NM passes between 60° and 70°, much closer to the 60°, so the correct answer is 61°.

25. 12 : First plug all of the numbers into the equation. $2^2 + (2(5) - 8) \times 4$. Then follow the order of operations.

$$2^2 + (2(5) - 8) \times 4 =$$
$$2^2 + 2 \times 4 =$$
$$4 + 2 \times 4 =$$
$$4 + 8 = 12$$

26. C: First add the costs of all 3 books together to get $35. Then find out what 30% of $35 is. This can be done by multiplying it times .3 to get $10.50. Then subtract $10.50 from $35 and you have the sale price of $24.50.

27. D: The mean is just the average. To calculate this, find the total of all 10 numbers by adding. Then, divide that total by 10 because that is the number of data points. The total is 750, so the mean of this group of numbers is 75

28. B: Notice that the vertical scale should be 0 to 30 by 5's since each of the X's in the plot represent 5 students. Also, each column should represent a number from the line plot. For example, since Language and Sports Activities both show 5 X's, and each X represents 5 students, 5 times 5 = 25. The subjects of Math and Social Studies both show 4 X's, so 4 times 5 = 20. All of the values are found in this way and the only chart that shows these values is B.

29. A: Only this tree diagram shows all possible color combinations of one dark color and one light color, where the two options of a light color are shown for each of the three possible dark color options. So, there will be six possibilities altogether.

30. A: The appropriate fractions can be found by putting the amount of money spent on each category over the total amount of money spent. $\frac{50}{120}$ is a little less than half, since half of 120 is 60. $\frac{30}{120}$ simplifies to $\frac{1}{4}$ and $\frac{40}{120}$ simplifies to $\frac{1}{3}$. This means that Sammy spent almost $\frac{1}{2}$ his money on shirts, $\frac{1}{4}$ of his money on jeans, and $\frac{1}{3}$ of his money on school supplies. The graph in A best represents those fractions.

31. B: Since each person is paid by the number of miles driven, one must know not the total miles for the trip, but the miles each person drove. The fuel, weight, or hours do not matter for this problem.

32. B: To answer this question, find the total number of bulbs required by multiplying 10 by 3. The number of packages of bulbs required can be found by dividing this total number of bulbs, 30, by 5, to find that 6 packages are needed. Then, multiplying 6 by the cost per package, 8, we find that the total cost for all the bulbs needed was $48.

33. D: To answer this question, the total number of caps sold must be found by dividing the total sales, 3,360, by the price of each cap, 14. 3,360 ÷ 14 = 240, so 240 caps were sold in total. So, looking at the graph, it appears that about half of the caps were white, around 120. The graph also shows that the other 3 colors were sold in about equal numbers, so dividing the other half, 120, by 3, gives around 40. Then, adding 120 white caps and 40 pink caps, gives an answer of 160. The club had close to 160 combined sales of white and pink caps.

34. B: First add all of the lengths together to get $43\frac{1}{2}$ inches. Then divide by 6 to get the mean. $43\frac{1}{2} \div 6 = 7\frac{1}{4}$

35. D: This procedure first finds the area to be fertilized, by multiplying the length and width of the rectangular yard. Then, it divides that area by the area each pound of fertilizer will cover.

36. D: $380 is 80% of $475, and answer choice D is the only one that represents this. s=.8r

37. 24: Begin by arranging the different weights from least to greatest:

48 lbs, 55 lbs, 61 lbs, 63 lbs 68 lbs, 72 lbs. Range is the difference between the highest and lowest values in a set of data; therefore, 72 − 48 = 24.

38. 6: To find the greatest common factor first factor both numbers completely. The factors of 66 include 1, 2, 3, 6, 11, 22, 33, and 66. The factors of 24 include 1, 2, 3, 4, 6, 8, 12, and 24. The greatest factor that they have in common is 6.

39. B: After the reflection and the translation the new point would be here:

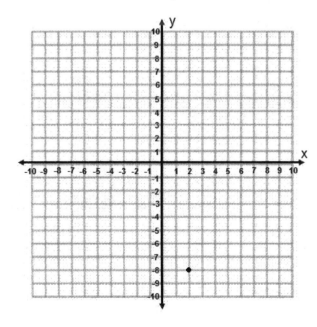

- 85 -

and that is the point (2, -8)

40. B: It is easier to think as the required 16 inches as 16.00 and convert all answer choices to a decimal to compare. Anything greater than 16.00 would be sufficient. $15\frac{7}{10}$ is equal to 15.7, $\frac{47}{3}$ is equivalent to 15.67 and 15.5 remains 15.5. These three choices are all slightly less than the required 16.00 inches; therefore making 16.25 inches the only adequate choice.

41. C: Since she earns $5 for walking dogs and watering flowers, this term can be combined to simplify the equation. The other terms for bringing back trashcans and checking the mail are straight multiplication.

42. A: To correctly write a percent as a decimal, the percent sign is dropped and the number is rewritten with the decimal point two places to the left. If there is not two digits in the percent, a zero is used as a place holder. This is because a percent is always a value out of 100 and the second place after the decimal point is the hundredths place. So, 8% = 0.08.

43. D: Each of the units represents $\frac{1}{4}$. The point Z is 9 units right of the y-axis or $\frac{9}{4}$ units, which is equivalent to $2\frac{1}{4}$. The point R is also 9 units from the y-axis, or $\frac{9}{4}$, which is equivalent to $2\frac{1}{4}$. Be careful to notice that coordinate pairs always come in the order of the x-coordinate and then the y-coordinate, and is defined by the pair of numbers. The y- coordinate for Z is $\frac{7}{8}$, while Point R has a y-coordinate of $3\frac{1}{2}$.

44. Part A: Count the number of customers in each age group and draw a bar on the histogram that represents that.

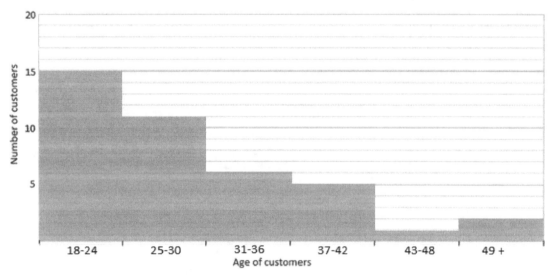

Part B: Yes: The median is the middle number of the group. Since there are 40 numbers there is no middle number so the median is the mean of the 20th and 21st number. Since this problem does not ask for a specific number there is no reason to write out the numbers and find the 20th and 21st. Instead you can see that the 25-30 age range encompasses numbers 16-26, so yes the median is in that range.

45. In this problem there are several pairs of numbers that can provide a correct answer. An *x* input of 0 would return a *y* of 4. An input of 2 would return a 6, and an input of 3 would return a 13. **(0,4), (2,6), (3,13)**

46. D: Antoinette bought 2 pairs of earrings at $10 each. To find the amount of money spent on the earrings, 10 must be multiplied by 2. Then adding that $20 to the $12 she paid for the picture and also adding $7 for lunch, she spent $39 in all. $50 – $39 = $11

Practice Test #2

Practice Questions

1. Four students measured the length of the pencil each was using. The list shows the lengths, in centimeters, of the four pencils.

17.03 cm, 17.4 cm, 17.31 cm, 17.09 cm

Which list shows the lengths of the pencils in order, from shortest to longest?

    a. 17.4 cm, 17.31 cm, 17.09 cm, 17.03 cm
    b. 17.03 cm, 17.09 cm, 17.4 cm, 17.31 cm
    c. 17.4 cm, 17.03 cm, 17.09 cm, 17.31 cm
    d. 17.03 cm, 17.09 cm, 17.31 cm, 17.4 cm

2. Castor collects only baseball and football cards. He has 40 baseball cards and 10 football cards. Which decimal best shows the part of his entire card collection represented by his baseball cards?

    a. 0.8
    b. 0.75
    c. 0.4
    d. 0.25

3. Which expression best shows the prime factorization of 630?

    a. $2 \times 3 \times 105$
    b. $2 \times 5 \times 7 \times 9$
    c. $2 \times 3^2 \times 5 \times 7$
    d. $2^2 \times 3^2 \times 5 \times 7$

4. Place the following numbers on the number line in the correct location:

$$-\frac{5}{3}, -\frac{2}{5}, 1.3, 1\frac{3}{5}$$

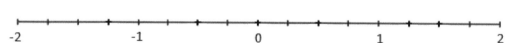

5. A club is making necklaces in school colors. They plan to use an equal number of blue beads and silver beads on each necklace. The blue beads come in bags of 60 and the silver beads come in bags of 80. What is the smallest number of bags of each color the club can purchase to have an equal number of each color bead with no beads left when the necklaces are finished? Explain why your answer is correct.

    a. 3 bags of blue and 4 bags of silver
    b. 4 bags of blue and 3 bags of silver
    c. 40 bags of blue and 30 bags of silver
    d. 80 bags of blue and 60 bags of silver

6. Evan measured the amount of rain in the gauge over the weekend. On Saturday, he measured $1\frac{6}{10}$ inches and on Sunday, $\frac{8}{10}$ inches. What is the total amount of rain, in inches, Evan measured on those two days, written in the simplest form?

a. $1\frac{14}{20}$

b. $1\frac{4}{10}$

c. $1\frac{2}{5}$

d. $2\frac{2}{5}$

7. Rafael purchased 8 new tires for the two family cars. The price of each tire was $144, including taxes. He agreed to make 18 equal monthly payments, interest-free, to pay for the tires. What will be the amount Rafael should pay each month? Explain how you solved the problem.

a. $16

b. $32

c. $64

d. $128

_____

_____

_____

8. Part A: In the graph below what is the area of the smaller figure? Each square on the graph is one square unit.

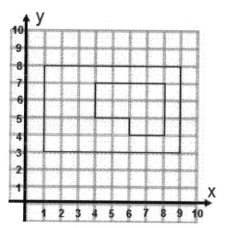

_____

Part B: The area of the smaller figure is what fraction of the larger one?

_____

9. William needs to find the value of the expression below. What is the value of this expression?

$$3^2 \times 2 - 4(3 - 1)$$

    a. 28
    b. 18
    c. 14
    d. 10

10. A farmer had about 150 bags of potatoes on his trailer. Each bag contained from 23 to 27 pounds of potatoes. Which is the best estimate of the total number of pounds of potatoes on the farmer's trailer?

    a. 3,000
    b. 3,700
    c. 4,100
    d. 5,000

11. Elena counted the number of birds that came to her bird bath one afternoon. While she watched, 20 sparrows, 16 finches, 4 wrens, and 10 jays came to the bird bath. Which ratio, in simplest form, compares the number of finches that Elena counted to the number of sparrows?

    a. 4 : 5
    b. 4 : 9
    c. 16 : 20
    d. 20 : 36

12. One cold afternoon at a small café, 20 people drank hot tea, 45 drank coffee, and 15 drank hot chocolate. Which ratio compares the number of people who drank coffee to the number who drank tea?

    a. 4 to 13
    b. 4 to 9
    c. 9 to 4
    d. 3 to 1

13. Part A: A lake near Armando's home is reported to be 80% full of water. Which fraction is equivalent to 80% and in simplest form?

    a. $\dfrac{1}{80}$
    b. $\dfrac{8}{10}$
    c. $\dfrac{4}{5}$
    d. $\dfrac{80}{1}$

Part B: If the lake is currently 12 feet deep, how deep would it be when it is completely full?

_____

14. The rectangle in this drawing is divided into equal-sized parts, with some of them shaded a darker color.

What percent best represents the part of the rectangle that is shaded a darker color?

    a. 8%
    b. 20%
    c. 53%
    d. 80%

15. Annette read that out of 20 televisions sold in her state last year, 3 were Brand V. If a furniture store near her home sold 360 televisions last year, about how many should Annette expect to be Brand V?

    a. 18
    b. 54
    c. 1,080
    d. 2,400

16. Gloria created a shape with vertices: $N, P, R,$ and S. She measured the angles formed at the vertices and wrote the information shown here.

$$m\angle N = 90°, m\angle P = 70°, m\angle R = 100°, m\angle S = 100°$$

Which of the angles Gloria created is an acute angle?

    a. $\angle N$
    b. $\angle P$
    c. $\angle R$
    d. $\angle S$

17. Thomas has mapped out his neighborhood on the graph below. He marked his house with the Point H, he marked his school with the point S, and he marked the park with the point P. Each square on the graph represents .25 miles. In the morning he walks to school, and after school he walks to the park. How far has he walked? Explain how you solved this problem.

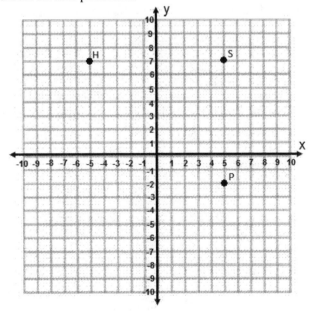

18. Jeremy put a heavy chalk mark on the tire of his bicycle. His bike tire is 27 inches in diameter. When he rolled the bike, the chalk left marks on the sidewalk. Which expression can be used to best determine the distance, in inches, the bike rolled from the first mark to the fourth mark?

    a. $3(27\pi)$
    b. $4\pi(27)$
    c. $(27 \div 3)\pi$
    d. $(27 \div 4)\pi$

19. The table below gives the positions of several terms in a sequence and the values of those terms.

Sequence

Position of term, n	Value of Term
1	1
2	6
3	11
4	16
5	21
n	?

Which rule can be used to find the value of n?

    a. 5n
    b. 6n
    c. 5n − 4
    d. 6n − 5

20. Julia has a cell phone contract with a monthly charge of $45. She bought a phone with a one-time price of $50 with that contract. Which table best represents the total of all charges which should be paid at the end of each month of the contract?

a.

Number of Months	1	2	3	4	5	6
Total Charges	$45	$90	$135	$180	$225	$270

b.

Number of Months	1	2	3	4	5	6
Total Charges	$95	$140	$185	$230	$275	$320

c.

Number of Months	1	2	3	4	5	6
Total Charges	$95	$190	$285	$380	$475	$570

d.

Number of Months	1	2	3	4	5	6
Total Charges	$50	$95	$140	$185	$230	$275

21. This table shows bases, heights, and areas of four triangles. In each triangle, the base remains the same and the height changes.

Triangles

Base, *b*	30 yards	30 yards	30 yards	30 yards
Height, *h*	20 yards	40 yards	60 yards	80 yards
Area, *A*	300 square yards	600 square yards	900 square yards	1200 square yards

Which formula best represents the relationship between *A*, the areas of these triangles, and *h*, their heights?

a. $A = \dfrac{h}{30}$

b. $A = \dfrac{h}{15}$

c. $A = 30h$

d. $A = 15h$

22. An automobile mechanic charges $65 per hour when repairing an automobile. There is also a charge for the parts required. Which equation can the mechanic use to calculate the charge, *c*, to repair an automobile which requires *h* hours and *p* dollars worth of parts?

a. $c = 65(h + p)$

b. $c = 65h + p$

c. $c = 65p + h$

d. $c = h + p$

23. Greg knows that in the triangle below, $m\angle X$ is 50° more than $m\angle V$.

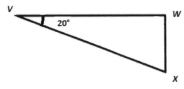

What is the measure of $\angle W$?

a. 20°

b. 50°

c. 70°

d. 90°

24. Silvia knows that in this shape, ∠**M** is equal in measure to ∠**K**, and that the measure of ∠**N** is 4 times the measure of ∠**K**.

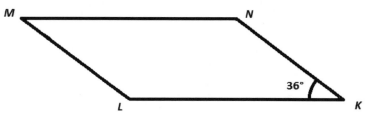

What is the measure of ∠**L**?

    a. 36°
    b. 72°
    c. 144°
    d. 288°

25. There are five points labeled on this grid.

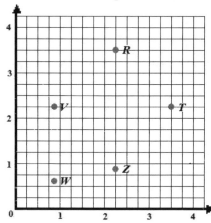

Which of the points on the grid best represents the point at $(3\frac{1}{2}, 2\frac{1}{4})$?

    a. R
    b. T
    c. V
    d. W

26. Curtis measured the temperature of water in a flask in Science class. The temperature of the water was 35°C. He carefully heated the flask so that the temperature of the water increased about 2°C every 3 minutes. Approximately how much had the temperature of the water increased after 20 minutes?

    a. 10°C
    b. 13°C
    c. 15°C
    d. 35°C

27. Carlos helped in the library by putting new books on the shelves. Each shelf held between 21 and 24 books. Each bookcase had 5 shelves and Carlos filled 2 of the bookcases. Which number is nearest to the number of books Carlos put on the shelves?

    a. 100
    b. 195
    c. 215
    d. 240

28. Several angles and a protractor are shown in this drawing.

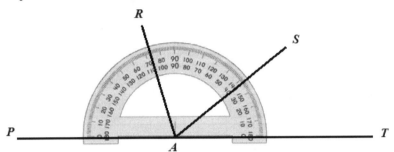

Which measure, in degrees, is closest to the measure of ∠**PAS**?

    a. 37°
    b. 43°
    c. 143°
    d. 157°

29. A lamp Sara decided to order online comes in four colors: brown, tan, white, and yellow. The shade for the lamp can be one of two styles: round or square. Which list shows all the possible combinations for a lamp of one color and one style for its shade that Sara can order?

    a.

| Brown, Round | White, Square |
| Tan, Round | Yellow Square |

    b.

Brown, Tan	Yellow, Round
Tan, White	Round Square
White, Yellow	

    c.

Brown, Tan	Tan, White
Brown, White	Tan, Round
Brown, Yellow	Tan Square

    d.

Brown, Round	Brown Square
Tan, Round	Tan, Square
White, Round	White, Square
Yellow, Round	Yellow, Square

30. Alma collected coins. In the bag where she kept only dimes, she had dimes from four different years. She had 20 dimes minted in 1942, 30 minted in 1943, 40 minted in 1944, and 10 minted in 1945. If Alma reached into the bag without looking and took a dime, what is the probability that she took a dime minted in 1945?

    a. $\frac{2}{5}$

    b. $\frac{3}{10}$

    c. $\frac{1}{5}$

    d. $\frac{1}{10}$

31. Jacob recorded the high temperature in his backyard each day for six days. The list below shows those high temperatures.

61°, 54°, 58°, 63°, 71°, 71°

Which of these temperatures is the median of the ones in Jacob's list?

    a. 17°
    b. 62°
    c. 63°
    d. 71°

32. Mr. Smith paid $60 for a kit to build a dollhouse for his granddaughter. He also paid $10 for tools, $20 for paint, and $10 for other supplies to build the dollhouse. Which graph best represents the dollhouse expenses Mr. Smith had?

    a.

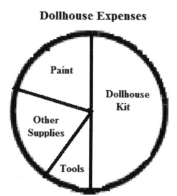

    c.

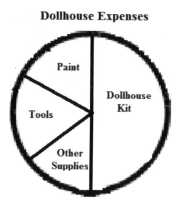

b.

Dollhouse Expenses

d.

Dollhouse Expenses

33. People who attended an orchestra concert at Johnson Middle School were asked to which of five age groups they belonged. The data is recorded in this graph.

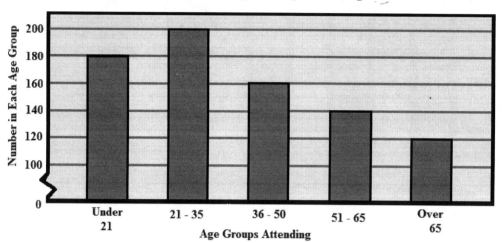

Which table correctly represents the data recorded in the graph?

a.

Number of Each Age Group Attending Concert

Age Group (in years)	Under 21	21 – 35	36 – 50	51 – 65	Over 65
Number in Group	180	200	160	140	120

b.

Number of Each Age Group Attending Concert

Age Group (in years)	Under 21	21 – 35	36 – 50	51 – 65	Over 65
Number in Group	180	220	180	160	140

c.

Number of Each Age Group Attending Concert

Age Group (in years)	Under 21	21 – 35	36 – 50	51 – 65	Over 65
Number in Group	180	200	140	120	100

d.

Number of Each Age Group Attending Concert

Age Group (in years)	Under 21	21 – 35	36 – 50	51 – 65	Over 65
Number in Group	180	200	160	120	120

34. Harlan plans to make stew for a large group. The recipe he uses requires 150 carrots. He knows that he can buy large bags of carrots for $3.75 each. What additional information does Harlan need to find the amount of money the carrots will cost for his stew?

a. The amounts of other vegetables he will need for the stew
b. The number of people he expects to eat the stew
c. The price each person attending the event paid
d. The number of carrots in a large bag of carrots

35. The cashier at Weekender Video Arcade recorded the number of tokens sold on Thursday, Friday, Saturday, and Sunday during one weekend. The graph shows the number of tokens sold on each of those four days.

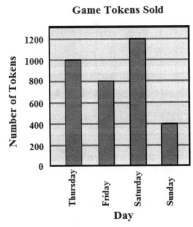

Game Tokens Sold

If the tokens sell for $1.25, what amount of money should the cashier have received for tokens sold on Friday and Saturday combined?

    a. $1,500
    b. $2,000
    c. $2,500
    d. $2,250

36. Part A: It took Hailey 18 minutes to jog from her house to the park. If the park is 2.5 miles away how long did it take her to go 1 mile?

_____

Part B: If she keeps the same pace how long will it take her to go from the park to her friend's house that is 3.5 miles away?

_____

37. Mr. Foster wants to put new carpet on the floor of his rectangular playroom. The playroom is 27 feet long and 18 feet wide. He has found an inexpensive carpet that is priced $14 per square yard. What would be a reasonable price for enough carpet to cover the floor of his playroom? Explain the steps you used to solve this problem.

    a. $486
    b. $756
    c. $1,260
    d. $2,268

_____

_____

_____

38. The rectangular floor of a garage has an area of 198 square feet. Andy knows that the floor is 7 feet longer than it is wide. What is length of the floor of the garage?

    a. 11 feet
    b. 14 feet
    c. 18 feet
    d. 92 feet

39. Timothy brought 12 of his toy cars to the baby sitters. These toy cars represent 30% of his toy car collection. What is the total number of cars in Timothy's collection? Explain why your answer is correct.

_____

_____

_____

40. Kenneth needs to repaint a wall in his bathroom. The wall is 8 feet high and 14 feet long. Part of the wall is covered with tile and he will not paint that part. The part of the wall covered by tile is 14 feet long and 42 inches high. Which expression could Kenneth use to find the area of the part of the wall he needs to repaint?

    a. $14 \times 8 - (42 + 8)$
    b. $14 \times 8 - (42 \times 14)$
    c. $14 \times 8 - [(42 \div 12) \times 14]$
    d. $2(14 + 8) - [(42 \div 12) + 14]$

41. Arlene had a garden for flowers. The rectangular garden was 10 feet wide and 16 feet long. In the garden, she planted daisies in a rectangular plot 5 feet wide and 10 feet long. She also planted pansies in a square plot 6 feet on each side. If Arlene planted no other flowers, how much area in her garden could still be planted?

    a. 13 square feet, because $2(10 + 16) - [2(5 + 10) + 2(6 + 6)] = 13$
    b. 38 square feet, because $2(10 + 16) - (5 \times 10) + (6 \times 6) = 38$
    c. 74 square feet, because $10 \times 16 - [(5 \times 10) + (6 \times 6)] = 74$
    d. 146 square feet, because $10 \times 16 - (5 \times 100) + (6 \times 6) = 146$

42. Tanisha bought 6 new binders for school and paid $4 for each binder. A few days later, she saw the same binders on sale at another store for 2 for $6. How much money could Tanisha have saved if she had bought the binders at the store where they went on sale?

    a. $6
    b. $7
    c. $15
    d. $18

43. There are five points labeled on this grid.

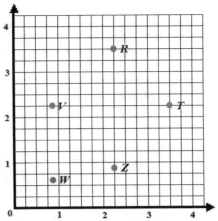

Which of the coordinates on the grid best represents the point R?

a. $(3\frac{1}{2}, 2\frac{1}{2})$

b. $(2\frac{1}{4}, 3\frac{1}{2})$

c. $(3\frac{1}{2}, 4\frac{1}{2})$

d. $(2\frac{1}{4}, 3\frac{1}{4})$

44. A fair was open for 4 days. The attendance to the fair during those 4 days is recorded below as well as the number of ride tickets sold.

Day	Number of entrants	Number of tickets sold
1	102	510
2	114	912
3	108	756
4	131	1048

Part A: How many tickets were sold per entrant on day 2?

_____

Part B: What is the average number of tickets sold per entrant over the entire 4 day?

_____

- 101 -

45. Paul was given the model below by his teacher and asked to shade it to represent $\frac{5}{8}$. He decides that he should shade 5 and then leave 8 blank and repeat this process until he is done. After he shades it she tells him that it is incorrect. Explain what the problem is and then shade it correctly.

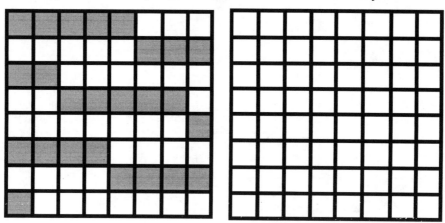

46. Xander was given 10 cups of birdfeed to pour into four birdfeeders. He poured 2 cups of feed into one feeder, 4 cups of feed into the second feeder, 2 cups of feed into the third feeder, and 1 cup into the fourth feeder. He did not put birdfeed anywhere else. Which expression best represents the amount of birdfeed leftover after Xander poured birdfeed into the four birdfeeders?

    a. 10 + 2 + 4 + 2 + 1
    b. 2 + 4 + 2 + 1 -10
    c. 4 – 10 + 2 + 2 +1
    d. 10 – 2 – 4 – 2 - 1

Answers and Explanations

1. D: To correctly order the numbers in this question, making the decimals all have the same number of digits by adding as many zeros as necessary to the numbers with fewer digits makes them easier to compare. Here, only 17.4 has fewer digits than the others, so add one zero to make it 17.40 (*this does not change the value*). Now, by comparing place values from left to right of 17.03, 17.4, 17.31, and 17.09, we see that 17.03 is the shortest, 17.09 is the next longest, 17.31 is the third longest, and 17.4 is the longest. Notice the question asked for shortest to longest, not longest to shortest.

2. A: In order to answer this question, we add the number of baseball and football cards to realize that there are 50 total cards in Castor's collection, 40 of which are baseball cards. To convert this to a decimal, we need to divide 40 by 50. This gives the correct answer, 0.8.

3. C: There is more than one way to solve this problem. One method is to use the fact that the number ends in 0. This means 10 is a factor. So, 10 × 63 = 630. 10 has prime factors of 2 and 5. 63 has factors of 7 and 9 and the 9 has two factors of 3. Putting the prime factors in order, least to greatest, and showing the two factors of 3 with an exponent of 2 gives us the answer: $2 \times 3^2 \times 5 \times 7$.

4. $-\frac{5}{3}$ is going to be slightly more than the $-1\frac{3}{4}$ mark on the number line. $-\frac{2}{5}$ is going to be a little more than $-\frac{1}{2}$ mark. 1.3 is going to be a little more than the $1\frac{1}{4}$ mark. $1\frac{3}{5}$ is going to be a little more than the $1\frac{3}{4}$ mark.

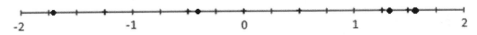

5. B: There is more than one way to solve this problem. One method is to find the least common multiple of 60 and 80. To do this, first find the prime factors of each number.

$60 = 2 \times 2 \times 3 \times 5$

$80 = 2 \times 2 \times 2 \times 2 \times 5$

The factors common to 60 and 80 are 2, 2, and 5. The factors that are not common to both numbers are two factors of 2 from 80 and a factor of 3 from 60. To find the least common multiple, multiply all the factors without repetition. That is, multiply the common factors (2, 2, and 5) and the other factors (2, 2, and 3) together:

$2 \times 2 \times 2 \times 2 \times 3 \times 5 = 240$

240 is the least common multiple. This is the total number of beads needed of each color. To find how many bags the club will need to purchase, divide this total by the number of beads that come in each bag for each color bead. 240 ÷ 60 = 4 (4 bags of blue). 240 ÷ 80 = 3 (3 bags of silver).

6. D: To answer this question, note that the fractions have common denominators. When adding fractions with common denominators, we need to add only the numerators, so, the sum of $\frac{6}{10}$ and $\frac{8}{10}$ is $\frac{14}{10}$. This should then be written as a mixed number, $1\frac{4}{10}$, which is found by dividing 14 by 10 which gives the whole number and the remainder becomes your new numerator over the same denominator of 10. The fraction $\frac{4}{10}$ can also be written as $\frac{2}{5}$ by dividing numerator and denominator by the common factor of 2.

Therefore, $\frac{14}{10}$ is equivalent to $1\frac{2}{5}$. Be careful here to remember the 1 from the original $1\frac{6}{10}$ amount given in the problem, which must be added to the $1\frac{2}{5}$ to make a total of $2\frac{2}{5}$.

7. C: First, multiply the cost of each tire, $144, by the number of tires, 8, to get $1,152. Then, divide $1,152 by the number of months, 18, to get the amount paid each month, $64.

8. Part A: 10: The number of square units inside the figure is 10.

Part B: $\frac{1}{4}$: The larger figure is 8 by 5 so it is 40 square units. So, it is $\frac{10}{40} = \frac{1}{4}$.

9. D: To simplify this expression, use the order of operations.

$$3^2 \times 2 - 4(3 - 1)$$
$$= 3^2 \times 2 - 4(2)$$
$$= 9 \times 2 - 4(2)$$
$$= 18 - 8$$
$$= 10$$

10. B: 3,700 is the only answer between the minimum number of potatoes that could have been on the trailer, 150 X 23= 3,450, and the maximum number of potatoes that could have been on the trailer, 27 X 150 = 4,050. Another method that could be used to answer this question is to multiply 25, the number halfway between 23 and 27, by 150. The product, 3,750 is very near the correct answer.

11. A: The ratio asked for is the number of finches compared to the number of sparrows. This compares 16 to 20, but the ratio can be written in simpler form by dividing both numbers in the ratio by 4, to get the ratio of 4 to 5. It is important to notice the order of the ratio. Since the number of finches is written before the number of sparrows, the ratio must be 16 to 20 and not 20 to 16. Also, note that the number of wrens or jays does not matter here.

12. C: The ratio compares the number of coffee drinkers to the number of tea drinkers, in that order, so the ratio is 45 to 20. Note that the ratio of 20 to 45 would be incorrect. The ratio of 45 to 20 can then be written in simpler terms by dividing both terms by 5 to get 9 to 4. Notice that the number of hot chocolate drinkers is not important in this problem.

13. Part A: C: The 80% means 80 out of 100, which can be written as $\frac{80}{100}$. This fraction can be written in lowest terms by dividing both the numerator and denominator by the greatest common factor of 20, to get the fraction, $\frac{4}{5}$.

Part B: 15 feet: If the lake is 12 feet deep at 80% full then you can just divide 12 by .8 to get 15 feet.

14. D: The number of shaded parts is 8 and the total number of parts is 10. This can be written as the ratio: $\frac{8}{10}$. Since percent is always a ratio with a denominator of 100, multiply both terms of the ratio by 10 to get the ratio: $\frac{80}{100}$, which can be written as 80%.

15. B: One method that can be used to answer this question is to write and solve the proportion: $\frac{3}{20} = \frac{V}{360}$, where V stands for the number of Brand V televisions that were sold at the furniture store. To solve the proportion, we can cross multiply: 20 times V and 3 times 360, which gives the equation: $20V = 1,080$. We solve this equation by dividing both sides of the equation by 20 to get $V = 54$.

16. C: Notice that there is a difference of 5 between the values in Column 2. This gives the "5" in front of n. Then, notice that if you multiply the position of the term by 5, the value is less than that product, by 4. So, the rule is $5n - 4$.

17. 4.75: Point H is located at (-5, 7), and Point S is located at (5, 7). The distance between these is 10 units on the graph or 2.5 miles. Point P is located at (5, -2). The distance between it and Point S is 9 units on the graph or 2.25 miles. So, Thomas walked a total of 4.75 miles.

18. A: The distance given from the top to the bottom of the tire through the center is the diameter. Finding the distance the bike traveled in one complete roll of the tire is the same as finding the circumference. Using the formula, $C = \pi d$, we multiply 27 by π. From the first mark to the fourth, the tire rolls three times, so we now multiply by 3.

19. C: Notice that there is a difference of 5 between the values in Column 2. This gives the "5" in front of n. Then, notice that if you multiply the position of the term by 5, the value is less than that product, by 4. So, the rule is $5n - 4$.

20. B: There is a one-time charge of $50 for the price of the phone and a $45 monthly charge in the first month for a total of $95. Then, a charge of $45 only is added for every month after that. Since the chart shows the total charge each month, adding $45 to the total due from the first month gives a total of $140 for the first 2 months. Then, $45 is added for the next month, for a total of $185 for the first 3 months, $230 for 4 months, $275 for 5 months, and $320 in total charges for the first 6 months.

21. D: The formula for the area of a triangle can be used here, but it is not necessary. To find the relationship between the heights and areas, look at the last two rows. A pattern can be seen that each value for the area, A, is just 15 times the value of the height, h. So, the formula is: $A = 15h$.

22. B: The amount charged for hours worked will require us to multiply the number of hours by $65. The charge for parts is not changed by the number of hours worked. So, the equation needs to show 65 times h, the number of hours, plus p, the price of the parts. So, the correct equation is: $c = 65h + p$.

23. D: To find $m\angle W$, we must first find the measure of $\angle X$. We know $m\angle X$ is 50° more than $m\angle V$. Since $m\angle V = 20°$, then $m\angle X = 20° + 50° = 70°$. So, $m\angle V + m\angle X = 90°$. It is important here to know that the sum of the three angles of any triangle is 180°. Since $m\angle V + m\angle X = 90°$, then $90° + m\angle W = 180°$. So, $m\angle W = 90°$.

24. C: Since we are told that $m\angle N$ is 4 times $m\angle K$, we can find the $m\angle N$ by multiplying 36° by 4 to get 144°. Knowing $\angle M$ measures 36° because it is equal to $m\angle K$ gives us the measures of three of the angles. The sum of the four angles of a quadrilateral always equals 360°. So, we add the measures of the three angles that we know and then subtract that total from 360°:

$360 - (36 + 144 + 36) = 360 - 216 = 144$. The measure of $\angle L$ is 144°.

25. B: Each of the units represents $\frac{1}{4}$. The point T is 14 units right of the y-axis or $\frac{14}{4}$ units, which is equivalent to $3\frac{1}{2}$. The point T is also 9 units from the x-axis, or $\frac{9}{4}$, which is equivalent to $2\frac{1}{4}$. Be careful to notice that coordinate pairs always come in the order of the x-coordinate and then the y-coordinate, which is why Point R would be incorrect.

26. B: The water temperature increased by about 2° every 3 minutes, or $\frac{2}{3}$ of a degree every minute. Multiplying the increase in degrees per minute by the total number of minutes yields

$$\frac{2°}{3 \text{ min}} \times 20 \text{ min} = \frac{40}{3}, \text{ or } 13.33°$$

Since the problem asks for the increase in temperature and not the total temperature that results after the increases, 13 is the closest to our answer.

27. C: First, since there are 5 shelves on each of the 2 bookcases, we multiply 5 by 2 to get 10 shelves total. Then, we find the minimum and maximum number of books that could have filled the shelves. Since 21 times 10 is 210 and 24 times 10 is 240, The number of books he shelved must be between 210 and 240. Answer D is 240, which would mean that every shelf was filled with the maximum number of books, which is not as likely.

28. C: Since segment PA lies along the left side of the protractor, we should read the outside scale. The segment SA passes between 140° and 150°, much closer to 140°, so the correct answer is 143°.

29. D: This list is the only one which lists all the possible ways Sara can order the lamp. Each of the four color choices can be chosen, and they can all be combined with one of two styles. In total, there are eight possibilities.

30. D: By adding all of the dimes, we find that there are a total of 100 dimes in the bag. 10 of them were minted in 1945. The probability, then, of choosing a dime minted in 1945 is 10 out of 100, which is equivalent to the fraction $\frac{1}{10}$.

31. B: To find the median of a set of data, first arrange the numbers in numerical order. Since this is an even numbered list, the two most central numbers are 61 and 63. Midway between these numbers is 62.

32. D: By adding up all of Mr. Smith's expenses for the dollhouse, $60 + $10 + $20 + $10, you find that his expenses totaled $100. Mr. Smith spent $60 on the kit, which is more than $\frac{1}{2}$ his expenses ($\frac{1}{2}$ of $100 would be $50), $\frac{1}{10}$ of his expenses on tools ($\frac{1}{10}$ of $100 = $10), $\frac{1}{5}$ of his expenses on paint ($\frac{1}{5}$ of $100 = $20), and $\frac{1}{10}$ of his expenses on other supplies. This is the only graph that correctly shows these fractions.

33. A: This table is the only one with the correct numbers from the graph for each category.

34. D: Since Harlan knows the cost of each bag of carrots, and also how many total carrots he needs, he also needs to know the number of carrots in each bag to find the number of bags he needs to buy. Then, he can multiply the number of bags by the price to find the amount of money the carrots for his stew will cost.

35. C: Though the graph shows the numbers of tokens sold on Thursday through Sunday, we are only asked about those sold on Friday and Saturday. So, we add those numbers together to get 800 + 1,200 = 2,000. Then, since each of the 2,000 tokens sold for $1.25 each, the 2,000 should be multiplied by $1.25 to get $2500.

36. Part A: 7.2 minutes: If it takes her 18 minutes to jog 2.5 miles then just divide 18 by 2.5 to get 7.2 minutes.

Part B: 25.2 minutes: If she keeps the same pace then it would take her 7.2 minutes times 3.5 miles. This equals 25.2 minutes.

37. B: It is necessary to find the area of the floor by multiplying the dimensions together. However, since the dimensions are given in feet and we only know the price of carpeting per square yard, converting the dimensions from feet to yards first is helpful. Since there are 3 feet in a yard, dividing each of the dimensions by 3 will give us the measurements in yards. So, 18/3 = 6 and 27/3 = 9. So, the floor is 6 yards by 9 yards, which is an area of 54 square yards. Last, we multiply 54 by $14, since each square yard costs $14 and there are 54, so the price of the carpet should be $756.

38. C: Guess and check is one way to find the correct answer. We know the length times the width gives the area of the garage floor, 198 square feet. We might guess that the width is 9. We know that the length is 7 more than the width, so, then the length would be 16. 9 times 16 is 144. We would see that our first guess is too low, so we guess higher. We might guess 12 for the width. The length is 7 more, so the length would be 19. 12 times 19 is 228, but this is too high. When we try 11 for the width, we find the length to be 18. 11 times 18 is 198, so the width of the garage floor is 11 and the length is 18. Be careful to note that the question asks for the length and not the width.

39. 40: If 12 of his cars represents 30% of his collection then divide by 3 to find 10% and then multiply by 10 to get 100%. $12 \div 3 = 4 \times 10 = 40$.

40. C: We multiply the length and wide of the wall to find the area of the entire wall. So, 8×14. Then, we want to subtract the area of the tiled section that does not need to be painted from the area of the entire wall. However, the height of the tiled section is given in inches, while all the other dimensions in the problem are given in feet. So, we must convert this to feet. Since we are going from a smaller unit to a larger unit (inches to feet), we want to divide. We need to divide 42 by 12 since that is the conversion factor (12 inches in 1 foot). Then we multiply the height (in feet) by the length to find the area covered by the tile. So, this is 14 times the 42 divided by 12. Last, we subtract the two areas to find the area of the part of the wall Kenneth will repaint.

41. C: The area of the garden should be found by multiplying 10 times 16 to get 160. Then the area of the daisy plot can be found by multiplying 5 times 10 to get 50, and the area of the pansy plot can be found by multiplying 6 times 6 to get 36. We then add the 50 square feet and 36 square feet to get 86 square feet, which is the area the two plots (daisy and pansy) cover. To find the area of the garden that can still be planted, subtract that from the total area of 160 square feet to get 74 square feet.

42. A: To find the answer, first determine the amount the binders cost at the different stores. At the first store, the price would be 6 times $4, since each binder costs $4, which is $24. At the second store, the binders are sold in twos. 6 binders would be 3 pairs of binders, and since each pair costs $6, $6 times 3 is the total cost of the binders at the second store, which is $18. We then subtract to find the difference, $24 - $18 = $6.

43. B: Each of the units represents $\frac{1}{4}$. The point R is 9 units to the right of the y-axis or $\frac{9}{4}$, which is equivalent to $2\frac{1}{4}$. Point R is also 14 units above the x-axis or $\frac{14}{4}$, which is equivalent to $3\frac{1}{2}$. Be careful to notice that coordinate pairs always come in the order of the x-coordinate and then the y-coordinate.

44. D: Only answer D correctly shows each amount of birdfeed being subtracted from the original total amount of 10 cups that originally given to Xander.

45. $\frac{5}{8}$ is not shading 5 and then leaving 8 unshaded. It is shading 5 out of every 8. The following model represents this.

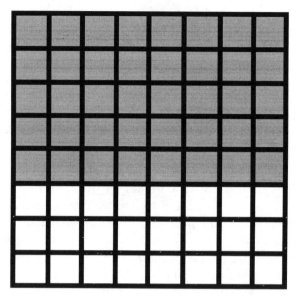

46. D: Only answer D correctly shows each amount of birdfeed being subtracted from the original total amount of 10 cups that originally given to Xander.

Science

Scientific Method

The Steps of the Scientific Method

1. Find a topic to investigate. Usually this is in the form of a question. For example, what is the effect of the pH level of the soil on plants?
2. Gather information about the topic. Read books. Search for information on the Internet. Ask an expert. Narrow the broad topic into a specific topic. For example, what is the effect of the pH level of the soil on the growth of grass?
3. Form a hypothesis or an educated guess. Try to answer the question based on the information that was gathered during the research. For example, I think that grass will grow the tallest in a soil that is slightly basic.
4. Design and perform an experiment to test the hypothesis. Experiments have an independent variable, dependent variable, several constants and a control if possible. For example, the type of containers, soil, and grass plants as well as the amount of water and sunlight are the same for every trial of the experiment. Only the pH of the soil varies or changes.
5. Record the data during the experiment. Then study or analyze the data to determine the relationship between the independent variable and the dependent variable. This usually includes tables, charts, and graphs.
6. State the conclusion. Do the results support or contradict the original hypothesis?

Purpose and design of a good experiment

An experiment tests the hypothesis to discover if the hypothesis is true or false. An experiment includes an independent variable, a dependent variable, a control if possible, and several constants. The independent variable is the factor that is changed or varied during the experiment. The dependent variable is the factor that is measured during the experiment. The control is the group of the experiment that is not under the influence of the independent variable. The control is used for comparison. For example, for the hypothesis, "If grass is planted in soil with a slightly basic pH, then the grass will grow the tallest," the independent variable is the pH of the soil. The dependent variable is the height of the grass plant. The constants are factors that remain the same for all trials of the experiment including the control. A good experiment has numerous trials at each variation of the independent variable.

Example

Describe an experiment to test the hypothesis, "If grass is planted in soil with a slightly basic pH, then the grass will grow the tallest."

Hypothesis - If grass is planted in soil with a slightly basic pH, then the grass will grow the tallest.

The independent variable is the pH of the soil. The dependent variable is the height of the grass plants. The constants include the type of pot, type of soil, type of grass seed, temperature, humidity, and the amount of water and sunlight. Forty grass seeds are divided into four groups of ten. Group 1 (the control group) is planted in neutral soil. Group 2 is planted in slightly basic soil. Group 3 is planted in a more basic soil. Group 4 is planted in a slightly acidic soil. The heights of the plants are recorded in millimeters every three days for six weeks.

Reasoning Test

1. ***Don't be scared by science terms or jargon.*** For many of the passages, you might not need to completely understand what is written in the paragraphs. Many of the questions are based only on your ability to read and take information from the graphs, charts, tables, figures, or illustrations.
2. ***The easiest questions usually come right after the passages.*** After quickly reading the passage and skimming the charts or illustrations, see if you can answer the first question from each passage.
3. ***Keep moving.*** Don't spend more than one minute on any question. Keep moving. The easy questions are worth as many points as the harder questions. By spending too much time on the harder questions, you will miss the chance to gain points by answering the easy questions associated with passages you will never even read before the time is up.
4. ***Work on the type of passages you think are the easiest first.*** Be prepared. Know the types of passages and questions covered on this test. Read the passages you feel the most comfortable with first.
5. ***Look for patterns or trends.*** When you read through the passage and glance over the charts and figures, look for patterns or trends. As one variable increases, does the other variable increase or decrease? How does changing one factor affect another factor?

Topics and types of passages covered on the Science Reasoning Test

The Science Reasoning Test covers a variety of science topics, including biology such as information about what affects the growth of plants, chemistry such as the pH scale, physics such as the effects of forces on motion, geology such as the different types of minerals, and astronomy such as information about the planets. Students are not expected to know specific or detailed knowledge of each topic. Instead, this test is designed to test your ability to read a scientific passage and find information from the charts, tables, graphs, and illustrations provided with the passage. Difficult terms are usually defined in the passage. Formulas are usually provided.

The Science Reasoning Test includes three types of passages: data representation, research summaries, and conflicting viewpoints. In the data representation passages, a paragraph or paragraphs with charts, tables, figures, or illustrations are provided about a specific science topic. Students are expected to understand the passage and interpret the information in the chart, graphs, and other visual representations. In the research summary passages, details regarding an experiment and the data from that experiment are provided. Students need to understand, analyze, and interpret graphs and tables. Students need to understand the design of the experiment and interpret the results of the experiment. Students may be asked to make predictions or inferences. In the conflicting viewpoint passages, two or more opinions are presented about a scientific topic. Students need to recognize similarities and differences between the viewpoints.

Science Reasoning Test

Types of questions on the Science Reasoning Test

Each passage contains a paragraph and usually charts, tables, graphs, illustrations, or figures. This test is designed to test your ability to understand and use the information that is presented in the graphs and charts. To answer a question, you may simply need to read a term from a table or read data from a graph. The more difficult questions may ask for you to recognize patterns or trends. You may need to combine information from the graphs and charts in order to answer a question. Complex math calculations are not required. Usually you can use estimation to get a close answer and then select from the answers provided in the answer choices. You may have to draw inferences or make predictions from graphs and figures or interpret coordinating tables.

Strategies for approaching the data representation passages

Tips for the Data Representation Passages

1. ***Don't be afraid of science passages.*** You don't have to completely understand the passages to answer the questions. Even if the terms and concepts seem complex, the questions are usually pretty straightforward.
2. ***Usually the easiest questions are first***. After quickly reading the passage and skimming the charts or illustrations, see if you can answer the first question associated with each passage. Usually the easiest questions are first.
3. ***Keep moving!*** Don't spend more than one minute on any particular question. If you don't know the answer, guess and move on. By spending too much time on the harder questions, you will miss the opportunity to gain points by answering the easy questions associated with passages you will never reach before the time is up.
4. ***Restate the problem in your own words***. Ask yourself what information is needed. Find the information you need to answer the question.
5. ***Look for patterns.*** When you read through the passage and glance over the charts and figures, look for patterns or trends. Does one variable increase as another variable increases? Or does one variable decrease as another variable increases? Is there a direct or inverse relationship or variation? Is there a pattern? Are there any highs (maximums) or lows (minimums)?
6. ***Stick with the information in the passage.*** Don't use any outside science knowledge in answering the actual question. This science knowledge may help you understand the passage, but all the answers should be in the passage or inferred from the passage.

Example

Partial Passage and Information from Diagram of Human Skeleton: An adult skeleton has 206 bones. The skeleton has two major divisions: the axial skeleton and the appendicular skeleton. Bones in the leg and foot include the femur, patella, tibia, fibula, tarsals, metatarsals, and phalanges. Bones in the arms and hand include the humerus, radius, ulna, carpals, metacarpals, and phalanges.

Question: Which of the following bones is not associated with the leg?

    a. Femur
    b. Tibia
    c. Patella
    d. Radius

Suggested Approach: Study the diagram of the skeleton. The radius is a bone in the lower arm. The femur, tibia, and patella are located in the leg. Therefore, choice C is correct.

Example

Partial Passage: Calcium is needed for healthy bones and teeth. Calcium is stored in the bones. By the time a person is a young adult, his or her bone mass is the greatest it will ever be. This is called the peak bone mass. As a person becomes an older adult, his or her bone mass decreases significantly. *Shown in the graph:* Bone mass versus age in years for males and females. Highest point on graph for males is near 30 years old and for females near 35 years old.

Question: At approximately what age do males reach their peak bone mass?

a. 10
b. 20
c. 30
d. 50

Suggested Approach: This question can be answered without even reading the passage. Often the first question following a passage is the simplest and can be answered from the accompanying graphs or charts. According to the figure, males reach their peak bone mass at approximately age 30. Females peak around age 35. Therefore, choice C is correct.

Research Summary Passages

What to expect in the research summary passages

In the research summary passages, details regarding an experiment and the data from that experiment are provided. Students need to understand, analyze, and interpret graphs and tables. Students need understand the design of the experiment and interpret the results of the experiment. Students may be asked to make predictions or inferences or to extrapolate. When reading about the experiment, ask these questions. What is being tested? Why is it being tested? What are the variables? What factors stay the same? Identify the independent variable and the dependent variable. Try to determine the relationship between these variables. Is there a direct relationship? Is there an inverse relationship? Be prepared to interpret data points and extrapolate data from tables and graphs. Remember, many of the questions can be answered by interpreting the charts and graphs without even reading the passage. When studying the graphs and charts, be sure to read all captions, keys, and labels. Identify axes and units.

Example

Partial Experiment Passage: Students studied the effect of the pH level of the soil on the growth of grass. The pH of the soil was varied between a pH of 6.0 and 8.0. Ten identical grass seeds were planted in each pot. The seeds were watered with equal amounts for a total of 14 days. The height of each grass plant was measured after 14 days and recorded in millimeters.

Question: Which of the following is the independent variable for this experiment?

a. The type of grass seed
b. The amount of water
c. The pH of the soil
d. The height of the grass

Suggested Approach: The independent variable is the variable that is changed or varied by the students performing the experiment. The dependent variable is the variable that is measured. In this experiment, the students varied the pH of the soil. The height of the grass plants was measured. Therefore, choice C is correct.

Conflicting Viewpoint Passage

What to expect in the conflicting viewpoint passage

In the conflicting viewpoint passages, two or more opinions are presented about a scientific topic. Usually the opinions have very specific differences. The opinions or viewpoints also share a few common ideas. Students need to recognize similarities and differences between the viewpoints. Some questions will cover specific details about the viewpoints. Students might be asked to make inferences or draw reasonable conclusions from the information that is provided. Some questions may ask which statements

- 112 -

both or all of the viewpoints agree with or who might agree or disagree with a particular statement. Only one of these types of passages is on this test.

Tips for Approaching the Conflicting Viewpoint Passage
1. **It doesn't matter who's right!** When reading the opposing or conflicting viewpoints, stick to the facts in the passage. Don't worry about who you think is right or wrong.
2. **Ignore your own opinion!** Your viewpoint doesn't matter. Just read the passage and get the needed information to answer the questions.
3. **Take shorthand notes.** Jot down or underline the information that supports each viewpoint. Jot down or circle key points of each viewpoint. Only use information that is stated in the viewpoints.
4. **Look for similarities and differences.** Ask yourself how the conflicting viewpoints disagree about the same concept or explain the same concept.

Example

Partial Passage: The Endangered Species Act provides for the conservation of ecosystems that contain the habitats of endangered species. *Scientist A:* The Endangered Species Act is effective is restoring species that were previously endangered. The act makes the public aware and concerned about endangered species. *Scientist B:* While the Endangered Species Act is effective in restoring species that were previously endangered, the act is too expensive to implement and too extreme.

Question: Which of the following statements would both of the scientists agree with?

a. The Endangered Species Act is too expensive to implement.
b. The Endangered Species Act is effective in restoring species.
c. The Endangered Species Act is too extreme as it is currently written.
d. Man has a responsibility to preserve rare species at all costs.

Suggested Approach: Since the scientists have extremely different viewpoints, the statement they might both agree with will be a general statement about the topic. These statements are often located in the beginning of the passages. In the opening sentences, both scientists state that the Endangered Species Acts has been effective in restoring species. Therefore, choice B is correct.

Example

Partial Passage: The Endangered Species Act provides for the conservation of ecosystems that contain the habitats of endangered species. *Scientist A:* This act is responsible for maintaining the natural habitat of many species. It is man's responsibility to preserve rare species at all costs. The Endangered Species Act has saved many animals, including alligators, whooping cranes, and bald eagles.

Question: Which of the following statements would Scientist A be most likely to disagree with?

a. The Endangered Species Act helped save the bald eagle.
b. The Endangered Species Act preserves habitats of numerous species.
c. The Endangered Species Act should be enforced at all costs.
d. The Endangered Species Act is too expensive and too extreme.

Suggested Approach: Before reading any of the questions, read through all the passages. Underline key points and jot down notes in the margins. When you see the question is specifically about Scientist A, glance over the underlined parts and notes from that passage. Scientist A stresses the importance of preserving species regardless of the costs. Therefore, choice D is correct.

Practice Test

Practice Questions

Use the following information for Questions 1-6.

Students used a graduated cylinder (see Figure 1) to study the densities of liquids, including honey, corn syrup, vegetable oil, and water, as well as of several solid objects. Fluids or solid objects float in liquids that are denser. Fluids or solid objects sink in liquids that are less dense.

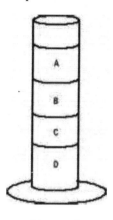

Figure 1

Experiment 1

Students prepared a density column by slowly pouring 100 ml each of honey, corn syrup, vegetable oil, and water one at a time into the graduated cylinder. The liquids formed four separate layers (A, B, C, and D) in the graduated cylinder. The densities of these liquids are shown in Table 1.

Table 1	
Substance	Density (g/cm³)
honey	1.42
corn syrup	1.33
vegetable oil	0.92
water	1.00

Experiment 2

Students dropped small solid objects of various materials, including aluminum, balsa wood, coal, and rubber, into the density column one at a time. The densities of these substances are shown in Table 2.

Table 2	
Substance	Density (g/cm³)
aluminum	2.70
balsa wood	0.16
coal	1.20
rubber	0.92

- 114 -

1. Which of the following statements is true?

  a. Corn syrup is less dense than vegetable oil.
  b. Honey is less dense than vegetable oil.
  c. Water is less dense than corn syrup.
  d. Honey is less dense than water.

2. Which of the following correctly lists the layers of the density column from top to bottom?

  a. Corn syrup, vegetable oil, water, honey
  b. Vegetable oil, water, corn syrup, honey
  c. Honey, corn syrup, water, vegetable oil
  d. Water, vegetable oil, honey, corn syrup

3. Which of these objects would be most likely to sink to the bottom of the density column?

  a. Aluminum paperclip
  b. Rubber band
  c. A small piece of coal
  d. Balsa wood

4. During Experiment 2, what is the most likely location of the piece of coal?

  a. Floating on top of layer A
  b. Floating on top of layer B
  c. Floating on top of layer C
  d. Floating on top of layer D

5. In another experiment, the students drop a small object of an unknown substance into the density column. If this object floats on top of layer D, what may the students conclude?

  a. The object has a density less than 0.92 g/cm³.
  b. The object has a density less than 1.00 g/cm³.
  c. The object has a density less than 1.33 g/cm³.
  d. The object has a density less than 1.42 g/cm³.

6. In another experiment, the students drop a small object of an unknown substance into the density column. If the object floats in a position located above the piece of coal, which of the following is most likely true?

  a. The density of the object is greater than 0.92 g/cm³.
  b. The density of the object is greater than 1.20 g/cm³.
  c. The density of the object is greater than 1.33 g/cm³.
  d. The density of the object is greater than 1.42 g/cm³.

Use the following information for Questions 7-12 Weather.

Clouds form when tiny droplets of water condense in the sky. When an air mass rises and expands, it cools. As the air cools, it becomes saturated with water vapor. When the temperature drops below the dew point, microscopic water droplets condense on tiny particles such as dust or soot. Cirrus clouds have tiny ice crystals. Meteorologists use ten basic classifications for clouds. See Figure 1. Clouds are named using the Latin roots in Table 1.

Table 1		
Latin Root	**Latin Meaning**	**Today's Description**

Alto	High	Higher than similar clouds
Cirrus	Curling lock of hair	Thin and wispy
Cumulus	Heap or pile	Puffy like cotton
Nimbus	Dark cloud	Produces rain
Stratus	Layer	Flat and horizontal

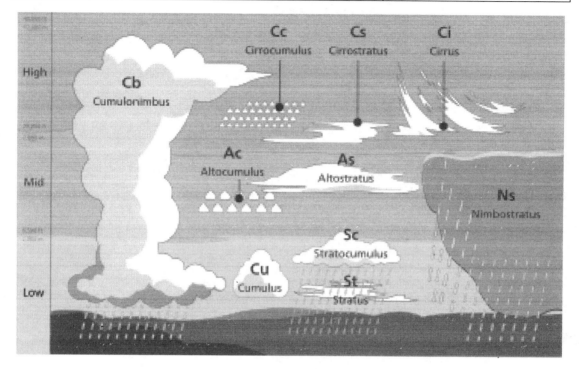

Figure 1

7. According to Table 1, which of the following clouds is associated with rain?

    a. Cumulus
    b. Altostratus
    c. Cirrocumulus
    d. Nimbostratus

8. According to Table 1, which of the following cloud names indicates a cloud that is located higher in the sky than similar clouds?

    a. Cumulus
    b. Nimbostratus
    c. Altostratus
    d. Stratocumulus

9. Which of the following clouds are made of ice crystals?

    a. Cumulonimbus
    b. Cirrus
    c. Stratocumulus
    d. Cumulus

10. According to Figure 1, which of the following clouds would most likely be located the highest in the sky?

    a. Cirrostratus
    b. Altostratus
    c. Stratocumulus
    d. Altocumulus

11. Which of the following descriptions best fits cumulonimbus clouds?

    a. Wispy clouds of ice crystals
    b. Towering, puffy rain clouds
    c. Low, flat layers of clouds
    d. Small, puffy white clouds

12. According to the passage, which of the following best describes cloud formation?

    a. Clouds form when the temperature of dry air drops below the freezing point.
    b. Clouds form when the temperature of saturated air drops below the boiling point.
    c. Clouds form when the temperature of dry air drops below the dew point.
    d. Clouds form when the temperature of saturated air drops below the dew point.

Use the following information for Questions 13-18.

Organisms are classified as producers, consumers, decomposers, and detritivores. Producers are autotrophs, which are organisms that produce their own food through photosynthesis. Producers include green plants, algae, and phytoplankton. Consumers are heterotrophs that feed on the producers or other consumers. Consumers include herbivores, carnivores, and omnivores. Decomposers and detritivores obtain their energy from dead organic matter. Numerous feeding relationships exist among organisms. A food chain shows the decrease in energy from one organism to another. The producer receives energy from the sun. The primary consumer receives energy from the producer, and then the secondary consumer receives energy from the primary consumer. A food chain from the Alaska tundra is shown in

- 117 -

Figure 1. Combining all the food chains in an ecosystem produces a food web. An aquatic food web is shown in Figure 2.

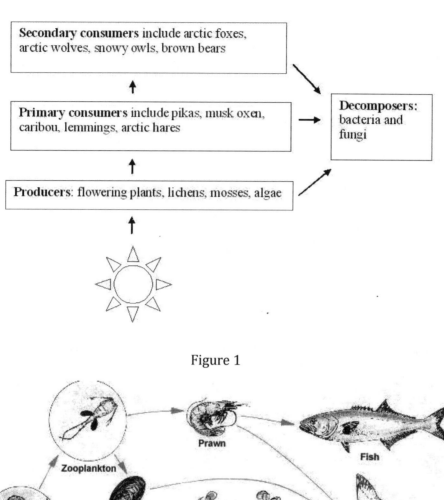

Figure 1

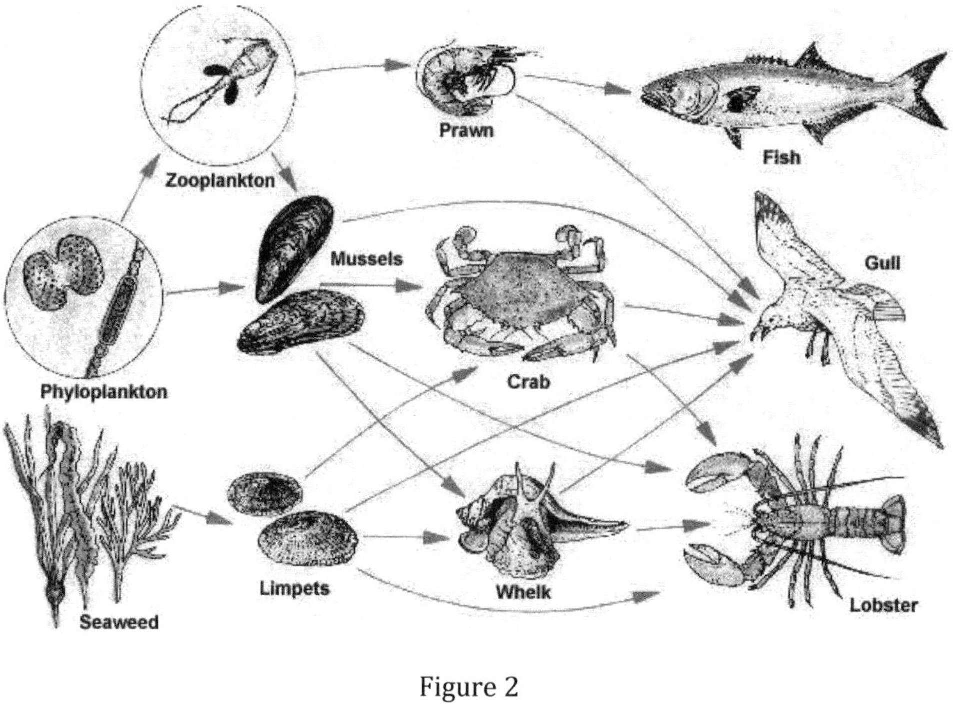

Figure 2

13. Which of the following is a primary consumer in the Alaskan tundra food chain?

    a. Lichen
    b. Brown bear
    c. Bacteria
    d. Musk oxen

14. Which of the following statements is true concerning the snowy owl from the Alaskan tundra food chain?

    a. The snowy owl is a detritivore.
    b. The snowy owl is a decomposer.
    c. The snowy owl is a heterotroph.
    d. The snowy owl is an autotroph.

15. Which of the following is the best classification for the grass in the meadow food web?

    a. Heterotroph
    b. Primary consumer
    c. Producer
    d. Detritivore

16. Which of the following food chains cannot be obtained from the aquatic food web in Figure 2?

    a. Seaweed, limpets, whelk, lobster
    b. Phytoplankton, mussels, prawn, fish
    c. Phytoplankton, zooplankton, prawn, fish
    d. Seaweed, limpets, crab, gull

17. According to Figure 2, which of the following classifications best fits the crab?

    a. Secondary consumer
    b. Primary consumer
    c. Producer
    d. Autotroph

18. Which of the following statements concerning consumers is not true?

    a. Green plants are consumers.
    b. Herbivores are consumers.
    c. Pikas are consumers.
    d. Prawns are consumers.

Use the following information for Questions 19-24.

Passage

Evaporation is the process in which a substance in a liquid state changes into a gaseous state. If water evaporates, liquid water changes into water vapor. Water vapor is the gaseous form of water. In order for a substance such as water to evaporate, the molecules near the surface of the liquid need to break free of the surrounding molecules near the surface. This might occur simply due to a collision with another molecule. The rate of evaporation is affected by several factors. Evaporation occurs faster at a higher temperature due to the higher kinetic energy of the molecules. Evaporation occurs faster over a greater surface area of the liquid due to the fact that at any given point in time there are more molecules closer to the surface. Air currents such as wind across the surface of a liquid will also increase the rate of evaporation. Lower atmospheric pressure also increases the rate of evaporation, because the molecules need less energy to escape from the surface of the liquid.

- 119 -

19. Which of the following processes correctly describes evaporation?

    a. Changing from a liquid to a gas
    b. Changing from a solid to a liquid
    c. Changing from a solid to a gas
    d. Changing from a gas to a liquid

20. What is the correct name for the gaseous state of water?

    a. Rain water
    b. Ice cubes
    c. Gas water
    d. Water vapor

Study 1

Students studied the effect of surface area on the rate of evaporation. Students poured 100 ml of water into a cup. The surface area of the water in the cup was 40 cm². Students poured 100 ml of water into a bowl. The surface are of the water in the bowl was 80 cm². Students then placed a fan blowing directly across the cup and the bowl. After 60 minutes, the amount of water remaining in each container was recorded in Table 1.

Table 1. Evaporation Study Data: The Effect of Surface Area			
Container	Surface Area of Water in container (cm²)	Initial amount of Water (ml)	Final amount of Water (ml)
Cup	40	100	70
Bowl	80	100	40

21. Which container had the largest surface area?

    a. The cup had the largest surface area.
    b. The bowl had the largest surface area.
    c. They had the same surface area.
    d. That information was not given.

22. How much water was left in the bowl at the end of the experiment?

    a. 100 ml
    b. 40 ml
    c. 70 ml
    d. 60 ml

Study 2

Students studied the effect of the temperature of the water on the rate of evaporation. Students poured 100 ml of water into each of two identical bowls. Bowl 1 was placed on the lab counter at room temperature. Bowl 2 was placed by the window in the sunlight. After 20 minutes, students recorded the temperature of the water in each bowl in Table 2. After six hours, the water remaining in the bowls was measured and recorded in Table 2.

Table 2. Evaporation Study Data; The Effect of Temperature			
Container	Temperature of water (°C)	Initial Amount of Water (ml)	Final Amount of Water (ml)
Bowl 1	20	100	90
Bowl 2	25	100	80

23. How much warmer was the water in bowl 2 than the water in bowl 1?

a. 20 °C
b. 15 °C
c. 10 °C
d. 5 °C

24. How much water evaporated from bowl 1?

a. 40 ml
b. 30 ml
c. 20 ml
d. 10 ml

Use the following information for Questions 25-30

Passage 1

Waves are back-and-forth motions that transmit kinetic energy. Most types of waves travel through matter. Waves transmit kinetic energy through the matter. The waves do not transmit the matter or the particles of the matter. The substance through which the wave travels is called the medium. Waves are produced when some type of force produces a vibration. The two major types of waves are longitudinal waves and transverse waves. In a longitudinal wave, the particles of the medium vibrate parallel to the direction of wave motion. See Figure 1. Sound waves are longitudinal waves. In a transverse wave, the particles of the medium vibrate perpendicular to the direction of wave motion. See Figure 2. Light waves are transverse waves.

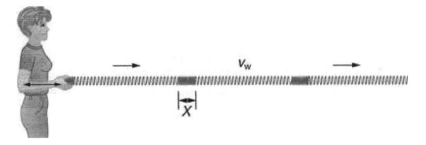

Figure 1

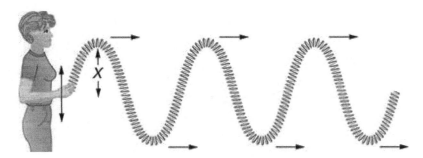

Figure 2

- 121 -

25. Which of the following statements is true?

    a. Waves transmit matter.
    b. Waves transmit particles.
    c. Waves transmit substances.
    d. Waves transmit energy.

26. Which type of wave is a sound wave?

    a. Longitudinal wave
    b. Transverse wave
    c. Neither a longitudinal wave nor a transverse wave
    d. A combination of a longitudinal wave and a transverse wave

27. A student ties one end of a six-foot rope to the classroom doorknob. She steps back until the rope is just tight. She then gives the rope a quick jerk upward. A wave travels down the rope to the doorknob. What type of wave does she produce?

    a. Longitudinal wave
    b. Transverse wave
    c. Neither a longitudinal wave nor a transverse wave
    d. A combination of longitudinal wave and a transverse wave

Passage 2

Sound waves require a medium to travel through. The kinetic energy of a sound wave is transmitted from particle to particle. Sound waves can travel through a solid, liquid, or gas. Sound waves cannot travel through a vacuum. When one person speaks to another, sound waves travel through the air between the speaker and the listener. The strength of a sound wave is referred to as intensity. The way the listener perceives the sound is known as loudness. Loudness is measured in decibels. The threshold of hearing which is the smallest vibration the human ear can detect is assigned a value of 0 decibels. A soft whisper measures at 30 decibels. A chain saw measures at 110 decibels. The threshold of hearing that is the loudness that actually hurts to hear is at 120 decibels. See Table 1.

Table 1 Loudness of Common Sounds in Decibels	
Threshold of hearing	0
Rustle of leaves	20
Soft whisper	30
Normal conversation	60
Hair dryer	90
Chainsaw	110
iPod at maximum loudness	115
Threshold of pain	120
Gunshot	140

28. Which of the following has the highest sound level?

    a. Normal conversation
    b. iPod at maximum loudness
    c. Hair dryer
    d. Chainsaw

29. In which of the following situations can sound not travel?

    a. In a vacuum
    b. In air
    c. In water
    d. In metal

30. What is the threshold of hearing?

    a. 0 decibels
    b. 1 decibel
    c. 2 decibels
    d. 3 decibels

Use the following information for Questions 31-35

Passage 1

The human body consists of millions of cells that require nutrients and raw materials to carry out their daily functions. Food provides the nutrients and raw materials for cells in the form of carbohydrates, proteins, and fats. Food also supplies vitamins and minerals essential for proper body function. Fats are used by the body in many ways. Fats store energy and are used to build cell parts. Fats also carry vitamins throughout the body. Some fats act as special messengers called hormones. All cell membranes are made of fat called cholesterol. Because the liver can manufacture many of the fats the body needs, only a small amount of fat should be included in the daily diet. Research shows that the consumption of certain types of fats leads to heart disease and other serious health problems later in life. One staple food source is eggs. Eggs are an excellent source of protein, vitamins, and minerals. Eggs contain a large amount of cholesterol, a type of fat linked to heart disease and other serious health issues.

31. According to the passage, which of the following nutrients is used to build cell membranes?

    a. Carbohydrates
    b. Proteins
    c. Vitamins
    d. Cholesterol

32. Which nutrient associated with eggs may be linked to heart diseases?

    a. Minerals
    b. Vitamins
    c. Cholesterol
    d. Proteins

Student 1

Student 1 states that the risks in eating eggs due to the high cholesterol content far outweighs any benefit that comes from eating eggs. People can get their needed protein from other lean sources of meat such as fish and chicken. Eggs can be replaced with low-fat alternatives in recipes.

Student 2

Student 2 states that the benefits from eating eggs, including the protein, vitamins, and minerals, far outweigh the risk in eating eggs. People need the protein, vitamins, and mineral provided by eggs. Eggs are a cheap source of protein as compared to lean meats such as fish and chicken. People should include eggs in their daily diet.

- 123 -

Student 3

Student 3 states that there are both risks and benefits from eating eggs. Eggs provide the body with valuable proteins, vitamins, and minerals. While eggs also contain a large amount of fat, their nutritional value is important. People should limit the number of eggs they eat every day. Eating one to two eggs a day provides the nutrients a person needs and limits the amount of fat consumed.

33. Which of the following statements would each of these students support?

    a. Eats are a healthy food source.
    b. Eggs are a cheap food source.
    c. Eggs are too risky to eat.
    d. Eggs provide needed nutrients.

34. Which of the students would agree that eggs should be included in the daily diet?

    a. Students 2 and Student 3
    b. Only Student 2
    c. Student 1 and 3
    d. Only Student 3

35. What suggestion does Student 1 make to get the needed protein every day?

    a. Eat several pieces of citrus fruit
    b. Eat whole grain bread
    c. Eat dark green, leafy vegetables
    d. Eat fish and chicken

Use the following information for Questions 36-40

Passage

Yeast is a single-celled, microscopic fungus. One type of yeast is used to make bread dough rise. When bread dough is rising, some of the starch is converted to sugar. The yeast ferments this sugar by converting the sugar into alcohol and carbon dioxide. This process is known as fermentation. The carbon dioxide is a gas that produces bubbles in the dough. Bubbles cause the dough to expand. This makes the dough light and porous.

36. What type of organism is yeast?

    a. Plant
    b. Animal
    c. Fungus
    d. Algae

37. Which of the following substances makes bread light and porous?

    a. Flour
    b. Alcohol
    c. Sugar
    d. Carbon dioxide

Study

Students studied the effect of temperature on yeast growth. Students poured equal amounts of sugar and yeast into three identical, empty water bottles. Students poured 150 ml of cold water at 5°C into the first bottle. Students poured 150 ml of warm water at 40°C into the second bottle. Students poured 150 ml of hot water at 105°C into the third bottle. Students then stretched a balloon across the top of each bottle as

- 124 -

shown in Figure 1. Students gently swirled the bottles to stir the mixtures. After 30 minutes, students measured the diameters of each of the balloons and recorded the data in Table 1.

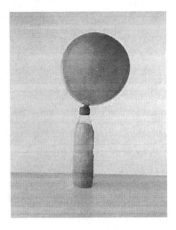

Figure 1

Table 1 Yeast Study Data	
Water Temperature (°C)	Balloon Diameter (Centimeters)
5	5.1
40	7.6
105	3.8

38. What was the variable in this experiment?

    a. The temperature of the water
    b. The amount of water
    c. The type of the container
    d. The amount of yeast

39. What was the diameter of the balloon at 105°C?

    a. 5.1 cm
    b. 3.8 cm
    c. 4.2 cm
    d. 7.6 cm

40. Which of the following statements best describes the data in Table 1?

    a. As temperature increases, the balloon diameter increases.
    b. As temperature increases, the balloon diameter decreases.
    c. As temperature increases, the balloon diameter increases and then decreases.
    d. As temperature increases, the balloon diameter remains the same.

Answers and Explanation

1. C: From Table 1, the density of water is 1.00 g/cm³. The density of corn syrup is 1.33 g/cm³. Since 1.00 g/cm³ is less than 1.33 g/cm³, water is less dense than corn syrup. Therefore, choice C is correct.

2. B: From Table 1, vegetable oil has the lowest density of 0.92 g/cm³ and forms layer A: Water has the next lowest density of 1.00 g/cm³ and forms layer B: Corn syrup has a density of 1.33 and forms layer C: Honey has the highest density of 1. 42 g/cm³ and forms layer D: Therefore, choice B is correct.

3. A: From Table 2, the density of aluminum is 2.70 g/cm³. Since this is a higher density than all of the densities (Table 1) of the liquids in the density column, the aluminum paperclip will sink to the bottom of the graduated cylinder. Therefore, choice A is correct.

4. C: From Table 2, coal has a density of 1.20 g/cm³. Since coal is denser than both vegetable oil (Table 1, 0.92 g/cm³) and water (Table 1, 1.00 g/cm³), the piece of coal should sink through these layers until it reaches the layer of corn syrup. Since coal is less dense than corn syrup (Table 1, 1.33 g/cm³), the coal should float on top of this layer (layer C). Therefore, choice C is correct.

5. D: Since the object is floating on top of layer D, the object must be less dense than honey, which has a density of 1.42 g/cm³ (Table 2). Therefore, choice D is correct.

6. A: If the object is floating in a position that is above the piece of coal in the density columns, then the density of the object is less than the density of coal. The density of coal is 1.33 g/cm³ (Table 2). The only choice that has a possibility of the object having a lower density than coal is choice A: Therefore, choice A is correct.

7. D: According to Table 1, the Latin root *nimbus* indicates a cloud that produces rain. A nimbostratus cloud produces rain. Therefore, choice D is correct.

8. C: According to Table 1, the Latin root *alto* means high. An alto stratus cloud is a higher-than-usual stratus cloud. Therefore, choice C is correct.

9. B: According to the passage, cirrus clouds are made of tiny ice crystals. Therefore, choice B is correct.

10. A: According to Figure 1, the highest clouds include the cirrocumulus, cirrostratus, and cirrus clouds. Therefore, choice A is correct.

11. B: From Figure 1, cumulonimbus clouds are tall and puffy; from Table 1, the Latin root *nimbus* indicates rain. Cumulonimbus clouds are towering, puffy rain clouds. Therefore, choice B is correct.

12. D: According to the passage, clouds form when saturated air drops below the dew point and tiny water droplets condense on tiny particles of dust and soot, Therefore, choice D is correct.

13. D: According to Figure 1, primary consumers in the Alaskan tundra food chain include pikas, musk oxen, caribou, lemmings, and arctic hares. Therefore, choice D is correct.

14. C: In Figure 1, the snowy owl is listed as a secondary consumer. In the passage, consumers are stated to be heterotrophs. The snowy owl is a heterotroph. Therefore, choice C is correct.

15. C: In Figure 2, grass is the first organism in all of the food chains that can be drawn from this food web. The first organism in a food chain is a producer. Grass produces its own food through photosynthesis. Therefore, choice C is correct.

16. B: According to the food web shown in Figure 2, the prawn is not a consumer of the mussels. Therefore, choice B is correct.

17. A: According to Figure 2, the crab feeds on either the limpets or mussels. Since the limpets and mussels are primary consumers, the crab is a secondary consumer. Therefore, choice A is correct.

18. A: According to the passage, green plants are producers, since they can make their own food. Therefore, choice A is correct.

19. A: According to the passage, evaporation is the process in which a substance in the liquid state changes into the gaseous state. When a substance evaporates, it changes from a liquid to a gas. Therefore, choice A is correct.

20. D: According to the passage, water vapor is the gaseous form of water. Therefore, choice D is correct.

21. B: According to the passage, the cup had a surface area of 40 cm², and the bowl had a surface area of 80 cm². The bowl had the largest surface area. Therefore, choice B is correct.

22. B: According to Table 1, the final amount of water in the bowl was 40 ml. Therefore, choice B is correct.

23. C: According to Table 2, the water in bowl 2 was at 25 °C, and the water in bowl 1 was at 20 °C. The difference between the two temperatures is 5 °C. Therefore, choice C is correct.

24. D: According to Table 2, bowl 1 initially contained 100 ml of water. The final amount of water in bowl 1 was 90 ml. Since the difference between 100 ml and 90 ml is 10 ml, 10 ml of water evaporated from bowl 1. Therefore, choice D is correct.

25. D: According to the passage, waves transmit kinetic energy. Waves do not transmit matter or particles of the medium. Therefore, choice A is correct.

26. A: According to the passage, sound waves are longitudinal waves. Therefore, choice A is correct.

27. B: This scenario resembles Figure 2. The waves produced in Figure 2 are transverse waves. Therefore, choice B is correct.

28. B: According to Table 1, the iPod at maximum loudness is 115 decibels. This is greater that the chainsaw, hairdryer, and normal conversation. Therefore, choice B is correct.

29. A: Sound is transmitted from particle to particle. Sound cannot travel in a vacuum since a vacuum has no particles. Therefore, choice A is correct.

30. A: According to Table 1, the threshold of hearing is 0 decibels. Therefore, choice A is correct.

31. D: According to the passage, all cell membranes are made of fat called cholesterol. Therefore, choice D is correct.

32. C: According to the passage, research shows that the consumption of certain types of fats leads to heart disease. The passage also states that cholesterol is a fat. Therefore, choice C is correct.

33. D: All three students state the eggs provide protein, vitamins, and minerals. Therefore, choice D is correct.

34. A: Student 2 states that people should include eggs in their daily diet. Student 3 states that people should eat one to two eggs a day. Therefore, choice A is correct.

35. B: Student 3 suggests that people get their protein from other source of meat such as fish and chicken. Therefore, choice B is correct.

36. C: The passage states that yeast is a single-celled, microscopic fungus. Therefore, choice C is correct.

37. D: According to the passage, carbon dioxide is a gas that produces bubbles in the dough, making it light and porous. Therefore, choice D is correct.

38. A: Students varied the temperature of the water. The temperatures used were 5°C, 40°C, and 105°C. Therefore, choice A is correct.

39. B: According to Table 1, the balloon had a diameter of 3.8 cm at 105 °C. Therefore, choice B is correct.

40. C: According to Table 1, the balloon diameter was the greatest at 40°C. The balloon diameter was smaller again at 105°C. Therefore, choice C is correct.

Reading

Literature

Explicit Information

Explicit information is the term for information that is directly stated in a story or passage. It is what the author tells you. It is not information that is hinted at or that you have to make a conclusion about. Explicit information can be facts or details about an event, something or someone. There is usually a lot of explicit information in a story and this information is often used to make an inference or draw a conclusion. To answer questions that ask about explicit information, simply reread the story until you find the answer. In fiction, details about characters, events, and setting are often explicit.

Read the following excerpt and tell what information is explicit:

> From his bed, Steve could see the moon begin to rise and the stars twinkle. He could hear the nurses as they walked down the long hall, their footsteps echoing in the quiet.

The explicit information in the excerpt is all about Steve and what he could see and hear. The passage says that he could see the moon begin to rise and the stars twinkle from his bed. It also says that he could hear the nurses walking down the hall. This is explicit information. The author is describing what Steve can see and hear. There is nothing that is hinted at in the excerpt except that Steve seems to be in a hospital. However, that conclusion is not explicit information. The author does not say this directly, so it is implicit information.

Inference

An *inference* is what a reader can deduce from the information in a passage. It is what the story may hint about, and what a reader can conclude as a result of what the author says in the passage. It is also the best guess that a reader can make based on what happened or was said or in a story. A good inference is based on or supported by details in the passage. For instance, if a passage says that Joan is holding her mouth and moaning, you might conclude, or *infer*, that she has a sore mouth or a toothache. You cannot be sure of this, but it is the best conclusion that you can reach using the information at hand. Inferences are considered implicit information. They are not found directly in a passage.

Read the following excerpt and tell what you can conclude about why Vicki got a cold:

> Hi Nance,
>
> Richard and I went camping last weekend. A bear ate all our food while we were sleeping. And it was cold and rainy the last night. We have both caught colds. Next time we go camping we are going to bring warmer clothes and extra food for the bears.
>
> Love, Vicki

You can conclude that Vicki got a cold because it was cold and rainy on the last night of her camping trip. She also talks about bringing warmer clothes the next time she goes camping, which further suggests that she was cold. However, the fact that a bear ate her food would have little to do with her getting sick, so that is not the reason she got a cold. It is logical to conclude that she got a cold because of the weather and not having warmer clothes. It is the best inference that you can make from the letter. Inferences are the best guesses that a reader can make based on the information in a passage.

Determining the theme of a passage

The *theme* of a passage is the message or lesson that a story teaches. It is what the author wants the reader to learn from the passage, and is the main point or moral that the passage carries with it. The theme of a passage may be stated explicitly, as in the case of a fable, but it is usually not stated. The reader has to combine the information in a story and what happens in that story together to figure out the story's theme. As the details of the story unfold, it reveals the theme; the theme is created through the story's development. The events of a story help shape the kind of theme the passage teaches. For instance, as you read, ask yourself if a character is doing something wrong and, if so, ask yourself if the character is punished at the end of a story. All of this combines to give a theme. Most themes are about life, society, or human nature. Themes also help give a passage unity.

Read the following passage and explain why "It is better not to run away" describes the story's theme:

> Ivan made fun of Sasha. So Sasha was scared of him. If he saw Ivan coming, Sasha hid. Then Sasha changed. He stopped hiding from Ivan. If Ivan laughed at him, Sasha laughed right back. He wasn't afraid anymore. Soon, Ivan stopped making fun of Sasha. This made Sasha feel happier.

The theme "It is better not to run away" fits what happens in the story. Sasha is scared of Ivan and hides from him. But then Sasha stops hiding and laughs back at Ivan, and after that he is not afraid anymore. For him it was better not to run away, but to stay and face his fears. In the end Sasha is happier. He solved his problem. This is the theme that the story teaches through the events of the story. Sasha and the reader learn that something good happened when Sasha did not hide or run away. This is the message of this passage. The reader needs to figure out the theme from what happens in a story.

Objective summary of a passage

A summary always includes the main idea of a passage and the most important details that are found in a story. It should explain what a story is about and then include the most important events that make a story different. In order to make the summary objective, you must make sure to reflect what the passage is about rather than how you might feel about the story. A summary should be fairly short. It differs from paraphrasing. *Paraphrasing* rewords the main idea but also uses many more details about a story than a summary does. Summaries allow the reader to remember what was most important about a story. Summaries do not include a reader's personal feelings or judgments about the story.

Read the following and explain why it is not a good summary:

> *Cinderella* is the story of a girl. Her step-sisters were mean to her. They wouldn't let her go to the ball. But she went anyway. She met the prince. I love the story of Cinderella. I wish I had a fairy godmother.

This summary includes some of the main idea of the story of Cinderella, that her stepsisters were mean and would not let her go to the ball but that she went anyway and met the prince. However, it leaves out the important information about her having a fairy godmother help her, how she lost her glass slipper, and the fact that the prince finally found and married her. These are all important details not included in the summary. It is also not a good summary because the writer included personal opinions about the story and a desire to have a fairy godmother. A summary should always be objective and not include personal feelings or opinions.

Effect of plot on a story's characters

The *plot* of a story unfolds as each event follows another, shaping the characters as they react to the various events that occur. The plot builds one event at a time and how the characters respond to what happens to them creates not only the plot but also the theme. Some characters are able to resolve their problems by the end of the story, while some characters fail to overcome their predicaments. Characters are revealed in their reactions to the events that take place. Some grow and some do not. It is for the reader to interpret the meaning of the story and understand its characters as they experience the events of a plot.

Read the excerpt and explain how finding the chest affects Marta:

> The map said this was the spot. Marta held her breath. Her fists were clenched into two tight balls. She lifted the shovel and scooped more sand out of the hole. There it was; she had found the chest with the diamonds. She opened the top. She would never need to work again. She smiled. It was really happening.

Marta finds the spot where the chest is. Her fists were clenched into tight balls. She was nervous. But then she saw the chest. She opened it and smiled. She was happy. Finding the chest would change her life. It was filled with diamonds so she would never have to work again. She was happy. This is how the event shaped Marta. It made her happy. Events can cause characters to have all kinds of feelings. Here something wonderful happened. Often, however, events in stories are not quite so happy. For instance, if a robber had suddenly seen Marta and the chest, he might have stolen the chest. Then that event would have had a very different effect on her. Readers need to look for hints about how characters are reacting to events, whether they are simply hinted at or stated in the story. In this way a reader will learn what characters are like.

Determining the meaning of words and phrases as they are used in a text

Readers can use *context clues* to figure out the meaning of unknown words and phrases in a story or passage. The clues may be found in the sentence with the unknown word or phrase in it or in the surrounding sentences. Many words have more than one meaning, so the reader has to examine the context in which a word is used. The word *sink*, for instance, has many meanings. It can mean to invest, to drop or go down, to go to a lower level, to go underwater, to lapse into a condition, to make an impression, and more. So in the sentence, "She was sinking into a coma" the meaning is clearly refers to "sinking" as the act of lapsing into a condition. Phrases must also be understood through context. In the sentence, "Clara felt she was a voice in the wilderness, but time proved her correct," the careful reader can figure out that the expression "voice in the wilderness" means someone expressing an opinion that may be true even if no one believes it.

Read the following sentence and explain how to determine the meaning of the word "unscathed:"

> Bill took a bad fall while he was hiking, but when he stood up he found he was unscathed, and went on to finish the hike.

The reader needs to find the context clues in the sentence to figure out the meaning of the word "unscathed." The sentence says that Bill took a bad fall. From this we could conclude that he might have been hurt. But it goes on to say that he was able to finish the hike anyway. So "unscathed" has to mean something like "unhurt." When trying to figure out the meaning of a word, substitute what you feel might be a synonym in place of it and see if it makes sense. In this case, Bill is clearly unhurt by the fall. By doing this you can figure out the correct meaning of unknown words or phrases.

Read the excerpt and explain how to determine the meaning of "spread like a cancer:"

> At first the army fought bravely, handily repelling the attackers despite being outnumbered almost four to one. But then it was learned that their leader Hector was dead, and fear spread like a cancer from unit to unit, changing what was once a proud and strong organization into a helpless band of stragglers.

The excerpt says that the army fought bravely and repelled attackers even though they were outnumbered. But the effect of hearing that their leader was dead caused fear to "spread like a cancer," causing this once proud army to become a band of stragglers. Certainly the expression "spread like cancer" cannot be a good thing; the reference to the disease also gives the reader a hint of what the expression means. If you substitute "spread very quickly" in place of "spread like a cancer," you will see that it makes sense in the context of the excerpt. This is a way to figure out the meaning of an unknown word or expression.

Figurative use of a word or expression

Figurative language is a literary device used by writers to expand reality by creating powerful and vivid images that keep writing fresh and appealing. There are many different kinds of figurative language, including simile, metaphor, personification, and hyperbole. *Similes* compare things using the comparing words "like" or "as." For example, the sentence "Anna is as graceful as a ballerina" uses a simile to describe Anna's grace. *Metaphors* compare things without using comparing words. For example, the sentence "Anna is a ballerina when she dances" uses a metaphor to describe Anna's dancing talent. *Personification* gives human traits to a thing or animal: "The music beckoned Anna to dance" personifies the music, which cannot actually beckon someone because it is not human. Finally, *hyperbole* is an exaggeration that is vivid but not literally believable. Saying that "Anna dances from the moment she wakes up until the moment she goes to sleep" does not really mean that Anna spends her every waking moment dancing; it is a hyperbole that describes how much Anna loves to dance.

Read the excerpt from a poem by William Blake and describe what form of figurative language it uses:

The wild winds weep,
And the night is a-cold;
Come hither, sleep,
And my griefs unfold.

The poem is an example of personification. In the poem, the poet says "The wild winds weep," thereby giving the winds the human characteristic of weeping. Later it says "Come hither, sleep," which is another use of personification asking that sleep to go somewhere as though it were a person. The poem gives the winds and sleep human characteristics. This is the definition of personification. It is not an example of simile because there is no comparison using the words "as" or "like." It is not a metaphor because there is no comparison between two things sharing a similar quality. And it is not an example of hyperbole because there is no exaggeration. The poem does contain some alliteration, however; the repetition of the letter "w" in "wild winds weep" qualifies as alliteration, which is another literary technique.

Denotative vs. connotative meaning of words

The *denotative* meaning of a word is what the word means literally. It is the exact dictionary definition of the word. The *connotative* meaning of a word, on the other hand, is what the word suggests. It is the feelings or emotions that the use of the word creates. Words often have associated meanings in addition to their dictionary definition. For example, the word "fragile" is defined in the dictionary as delicate. But another word meaning delicate might be "flimsy," but that word has many other connotations. "Flimsy" has a negative connotation while "fragile" does not. The connotative meaning of a word in a passage can be found by looking at the context clues in the surrounding sentences.

Read the following sentence and explain the connotative meaning of the word "palatial" and how it relates to the word "large:"

This house isn't really large, but compared to my apartment it seems palatial.

The words "large" and "palatial" both have the definition meaning of "big." But the word "palatial" means something that is not only big but also very elegant. This word expresses something far beyond just large; it emphasizes how impressive a thing is. The biggest hint to this word's connotations is the fact that it comes from the word "palace." This tells us that it is not just large, but regal as well. Another word that might be similar to "palatial" is "extravagant," but this word has a more negative connotation because it suggests something that is overdone. Words need to be studied for both their denotative and connotative meaning because the connotations that words bring up can flavor a character, setting, or event in a subtle manner.

Developing the theme, setting or plot

When a writer creates a story, she (or he) has to figure out the structure she will use. She has to include certain sentences that will give the reader information about the theme, setting or plot. She might use a chapter to set the scene for what will follow in the rest of a book, include a pivotal scene that will develop the plot or theme, or use a stanza that is filled with images that would help the reader of a poem understand the theme of the work. Writers of stories or poems want to develop their plot, setting and theme, so they have to come up with a structure that allows them to do so. It is up to the reader to analyze the work and to respond to what the writer has written.

Explain how the following excerpt would contribute to the development of the setting and plot:

His mother tied the cap beneath his chin. Then she pulled the zipper up on his coat as far as it would go. She put his gloves on. They walked the distance to the pond. The ice was frozen solid. "It's time to learn how to stand on skates," she said to her son.

The excerpt clearly sets the stage for the story. It gives the reader clues about where and when the action is taking place. The mother is dressing her son warmly. They walk to a pond. It is frozen. It is clearly winter and the mother is going to show her son how to skate. This excerpt not only tells the reader where and when it takes place, it also contributes to the plot. It introduces two characters. The mother takes time to make sure her son is warm, implying that she is loving. Her son seems passive. Because she has to dress him, he must be little. So a relationship is also revealed in the excerpt that will doubtless influence the plot.

Discuss how the following sentence would impact the theme:

Wanda realized then that she had made a terrible mistake and she would be haunted by the experience for the rest of her life.

This sentence would impact the theme because it suggests that Wanda would never recover from something that she did and that she would remember it for the rest of her life. This ties into a theme because it is saying something about life and what Wanda realizes about her life. We do not know what she did, but the sentence clearly states that it was a mistake. We would have to read the entire passage to understand why it was a mistake and why she would be haunted, but the sentence gives us a good idea that she learned a lesson from what happened.

- 133 -

Developing the point of view of the narrator or speaker in a text

An author uses many writing skills to develop a narrator's or speaker's point of view in a piece of literature. One way to develop a point of view is by having the narrator describe an event or a character. Or the author can choose to display a speaker's viewpoint through dialogue; a lot can be learned by what a character says. The manner in which the author reveals the narrator's or speaker's viewpoint may be subtle or it may be obvious. If it is done subtly, the reader will need to look for clues that help tell what the speaker's attitude is. That is why it is so important to study the language of the author, in order to analyze the narrator's or speaker's viewpoint about a character, event or topic.

Read the following excerpt and analyze the narrator's viewpoint of Bonita:

> Bonita always wanted to make a difference. So it was no surprise when she spent hours after school as a volunteer at the hospital when she was in high school. Then, in college, she tutored children at a local center and later worked as a nurse in Africa. She was special.

The narrator seems to like Bonita. He says that Bonita "always wanted to make a difference," and that it was "no surprise" that she volunteered at the hospital. To make his point even greater, he says that she tutored children when she was in college and later worked as a nurse in Africa. The narrator ends the excerpt by calling Bonita "special," so it is clear that he likes her. He would not say that otherwise. When determining a narrator's viewpoint of a character, be sure to watch for clues that tell you the narrator's opinion, such as the clues in this excerpt.

Analyzing the difference between reading, hearing or watching a story, drama, or poem

When you read a story, drama, or poem rather than hear or watch it, certain elements will be lacking. While the act of reading is a rewarding one, it is very private and subjective. When the same story is made into a video, a whole new range of senses are encountered. The characters will be real people and their actions and reactions to events will be that much more exciting. And the story will seem that much more real. Certainly hearing a poem read can be more powerful than simply reading it. Poets' words are meant to be heard and the effect of that language is much more meaningful when it is read aloud by a powerful speaker. As for dramas, they are meant to be heard or seen. Reading them is enjoyable, but subtleties are often overlooked. When a reader actually hears the dialogue of a play, it will have a deeper meaning. Seeing a drama brought to life is far more enthralling than reading it.

Comparing and contrasting a story about love and a poem about love

A story about love would involve characters and a plot. It would have events and probably a theme. It would look at love through the way the characters feel about it and what happens to them and what they say about it. In a poem, the speaker may be the only character. Rather than have a plot, a poem is much more likely to describe the effects of love in verse. Rather than having a conflict and events, a poem might be a tribute to love. Like a story, a poem would most likely have a theme. Some poems do have events and characters, but the emphasis is still on the language and, most of all, on figurative language. And a poem is much more likely to be read aloud than a story.

Historical novel vs. science fiction story

A historical novel is based on something that really happened; a science fiction story is not. A science fiction story is imaginary and probably contains components that are not based on reality. While a historical novel might deviate from the facts of a historical event by using fictional characters and dialogue, its basis is founded in historic fact. The science fiction genre only has fictional characters and

- 134 -

situations that might be set in the past, but more likely in the future. It has nothing to do with the reality of a time or period, or if it does, it is only in passing.

Informational Texts

Facts and details

Explicit information is the facts and details that are stated in a passage. It is found directly in a text rather than being suggested or hinted at. Explicit information is frequently used to support a main idea and can be found just by reading through a text, especially an informational passage. *Inferences* are usually based on the explicit information in a passage. When making an inference, the reader needs to put together the pertinent explicit information to form a conclusion that was not explicit in the passage. It is the best guess that a reader can make based on the information given in a passage

Read the following excerpt. Tell whether it contains explicit information or not:

> Oliver began to cut his way through the jungle. At first he was able to chop enough of the vines and bushes to make a narrow trail, but then the jungle became so thick that it was completely impassable. He had to return to camp and try to find another way to get to his destination.

Most of the information in the excerpt is explicit information. The information tells the reader about Oliver. It says that he was cutting his way through a jungle, but that the jungle became so thick that he couldn't get through and instead had to return to camp and find another way to get to where he wanted to go. All of the information is written right in the text. What is not clear is why Oliver was in the jungle and where he wanted to go. There is nothing in the explicit information to give us a hint about those questions.

Read the passage and discuss why the inference that the disease killed the elm trees is valid:

> Some years back, our towns were filled with elm trees. They grew tall and graceful. Some elm trees were hundreds of years old. Then a terrible disease came. Today elms are almost nonexistent in our towns.

When you make an inference, you need to look at the information in the passage. The passage said that years ago the towns were filled with elm trees. It tells the reader that the trees were graceful and some were hundreds of years old. It also says a terrible disease came and that today elms are almost gone. All of these details are explicit information. The reader can conclude from some of the information that the disease killed the elm trees. Using the facts that there were a lot of trees once, but not many today, you can infer that the disease killed them. This is not stated directly in the excerpt, but it is the best guess based on the information at hand.

Determining the main idea of a passage

Main ideas are what a passage is mostly about. It is the central idea of a text, the overall idea that a reader comes away with after reading a passage, and why the passage is written. A main idea is not a detail. Details in a passage may support a main idea by telling more about it, but they are not the main idea itself. Passages may have more than one main idea and paragraphs may have a main idea of their own.

Identify and explain the main idea of the following excerpt:

> People's permanent teeth should last forever. Unfortunately, many people don't clean them well. They don't brush or floss enough. They eat a lot of sweet foods. Because of this,

their teeth decay. Their gums become diseased. Some people have very few teeth left when they turn 60.

The main idea is that people don't take care of their permanent teeth enough. The author tells us this is various ways. The excerpt says that people don't clean them well and that they don't brush or floss enough. It also says that teeth and gums decay because of the sweet foods people eat. These are the details that support the main idea. The main idea is found in the details. When analyzing which statement is a main idea, make sure to choose one that has a broad message, not one that is talking about something specific.

Objective summary

An objective summary always includes the main idea and the most important details about the main idea. It does not include all of the supporting details. That would make the summary too long and more like a paraphrase of the text. A paraphrase includes a lot more information than a summary. When choosing which details to include, choose those that are most related to the main idea and are the most pertinent. Leave out those that are secondary. An objective summary does not include personal opinions; it is free of personal prejudice. It does not include judgments either.

Discover why the summary below is not objective:

> Many circus performers, like the lion tamer, the high wire performers, and the person who is shot out of a cannon, face dangers every day. But their love of the circus keeps them from leaving their jobs. That seems to be a silly choice to make in life.

This summary has a main idea and important details. The main idea is that circus performers face dangers every day. The details that are included are that the lion tamer, the high wire performers, and the person who is shot out of a cannon are among those performers who face the most danger. These are important details, so this part of the summary is excellent. But the summary is not objective because it also contains a judgment: "That seems to be a silly choice to make in life" has nothing to do with the main idea. It is the opinion of the reader and keeps the summary from being objective. Judgments and opinions that belong to the reader have no place in a summary.

Anecdotes and examples as a way of introducing, illustrating, or elaborating key ideas in a nonfiction passage

Examples and anecdotes are two fine tools for introducing, illustrating, or elaborating key ideas in a passage. Anecdotes and examples provide the reader with a concrete means of understanding what the abstract idea means in terms of daily lives. Anecdotes in particular make complicated notions accessible so that they are easily grasped by the reader. For instance, telling a personal story about yourself not being able to understand instructions might help to illustrate why putting together a bicycle is difficult to do. Examples can consist of quotations from authorities as well as first-person interviews and primary sources. All of this helps to enlighten a reader about main ideas.

Read the passage and explain the meaning of "corresponds to:"

> Computers can do a fine job of matching single people. They match people first on the basis of age so they will compatible. Most people want to date someone whose age corresponds to their own. Then computers pair off people by physical qualities like height, weight, hair and eyes.

To figure out the meaning of the phrase "corresponds to," the reader needs to look for context clues the same way the reader would try to figure out the meaning of a single word. The excerpt says that computers match people first on the basis of age so that they will be compatible. This is a context clue for the meaning of the term "corresponds to." Being compatible means getting along. Most people like to be with people around their same age, so this helps the reader decide that "corresponds to" means "resembles" in this usage. If the reader substitutes this word for the words "corresponds to," it makes sense.

Read the excerpt below and, using context clues, determine what the word "ostentatious" means:

> If movie stars wear too much expensive clothes and jewelry at one time, it makes them look ostentatious, which many people find unappealing because it makes the stars look cheap.

A good way to figure out the meanings of words and expressions without having to read their definitions in the dictionary is to use context clues. The way to discover context clues is to study the text. The excerpt says that if movie stars wear a lot of expensive clothes and jewelry at one time, many people think they look cheap. So the word "ostentatious" must link these two thoughts together. Wearing too much of anything that is expensive could be considered "showy." If you substitute the word "showy" for "ostentatious," it makes sense in the context of the sentence. This is the way you can work out the meaning of a word from context clues.

Figurative language

Authors often make use of a technique that is called *figurative language*. Figurative language allows the writer to expand the way in which he or she uses language. Figurative language uses words in a non-literal way; this means that the word or expression takes on a new meaning. For instance, an author might say that Anthony is like Superman. While, everyone knows that Anthony isn't really like Superman because he does not have super powers, the image of Anthony as Superman changes the reader's impression of Anthony. Figurative language takes many forms; it can be in the form of a simile, a metaphor, and personification. *Similes* compare things using the comparing words "like" or "as," for example, "Anthony is like Superman." *Metaphors* compare things without using comparing words, for example, "Anthony is Superman when it comes to helping others." And *personification* gives a thing or animal human traits, for example, "The future called out to Anthony."

Discuss the kind of figurative language used in the following poem by the Scottish poet Robert Burns:

O my luve's like a red, red rose
That's newly sprung in June;
O my luve's like the melodie
That's sweetly played in tune.

The poet uses similes to create an image in this poem. There are two similes used here and they make up the entire poem: he says that his love is "like a red, red rose" and that she is also "like the melodie." These are examples of similes because they use the comparing word "like" to compare two things. They are not metaphors because metaphors do not use the comparing words "like" or "as." The poem paints an image of the poet's love by comparing her to a red rose that has newly sprung and a melodie that is sweetly played.

Read the following passage and discuss how to figure out the meaning of the technical term "seismograph:"

> Karin knew this was a big earthquake, but she didn't realize how big until she started to check the readings on the seismograph. She was startled by what she read and quickly called Dr. Kai to alert him about her findings. They both studied the record carefully and then called the governor.

- 137 -

While a reader may not know the meaning of the technical term "seismograph," he could get a very good idea of its meaning from the context of the sentences around it. The first context clue is that Karin was checking the seismograph to find out how big an earthquake was, which must mean that a seismograph is some kind of scientific tool. She was startled by the findings of this machine, so it must have somehow managed to measure the extent of the earthquake. Through logic, a reader could figure out that a seismograph measures the intensity of earthquakes.

Connotations of "keen" vs. "passionate"

The word "passionate" suggests the state of being very involved in something, as in "liking something with a passion." The word "keen" is much less emphatic; someone who is keen about something likes it, but does not exhibit a passionate love of it. "Keen" suggests a mental state while "passionate" suggests an emotional state. Connotations carry many secondary meanings, so it is important to choose words that fit the situation. They are also filled with subtle overtones that should be analyzed and understood before choosing a word for use. Someone may be keen about a book or a dress, but it is doubtful that a person would be passionate about it.

Structure of a text

A good writer knows that every part of a text should fit together and have a purpose. For instance, writers often use a topic sentence at the start of a text to set the stage for the reader and alert her about what the topic is that the text will address. Writers use paragraphs to address different aspects of an overlying main idea. If the piece is long enough, chapters can be used to break up material so that it is more easily understood and found by a reader. There are other kinds of structuring a text too. A paper might be divided into sections for greater clarity. These techniques give writers greater flexibility and allow a writer to order a text in a logical and easier-to-read form.

Veronica has been doing a lot of research on frogs and wants to include data on several different kinds of frogs for a report. What kind of structure might be useful for Veronica to use?

The best choice for Veronica would probably be to divide her paper into sections, with each section having paragraphs that contain information about each type of frog. This would allow the reader to easily find information that he or she might be seeking and would act as a natural organizer for Veronica. She might include subheads with the name of each different kind of frog at the beginning of each section as well. She could also use subheads above a paragraph or a group of paragraphs, identifying the kind of information that is present there. And she could also include a topic sentence in each section or paragraph to tell what it is mostly about.

Determining an author's point of view

An author's point of view may be stated in a passage or it may be hidden or vaguely suggested. A student needs to read the text very closely to analyze what an author feels about her subject. When reading, look for any obviously emotional or opinionated statements. See what the author seems to have sympathy for. Some authors make their viewpoints very clear by stating it at the beginning or ending of a text, while others may want to keep their own opinions somewhat secret for many possible reasons. For example, many newspapers maintain a policy of unbiased reporting; even if a reporter has strong feelings, it may be nearly impossible to determine his point of view. Columnists, on the other hand, make their opinions very obvious. It is important to understand the author's viewpoint to ensure that you are reading something that gives a total picture of the topic without bias.

Read the following excerpt from a movie review and describe the author's viewpoint:

> The script, also by a newcomer, Alex Brandeis, is taut and suspenseful; however, the plot does seem to be a bit familiar. It's a story that seems to occur in the movies from time to time. Even so, this movie will leave you clutching your seat the whole time.

The author gives several hints about her viewpoint. First she says the script is taut and suspenseful, which suggests that she likes it. Then she says that the plot seems to be familiar, a sign that she is somewhat critical of the movie. She goes on to comment that the story has been repeated, but the final sentence makes it clear that the author's viewpoint about the movie is positive because she says "this movie will leave you clutching your seat the whole time." To determine an author's viewpoint, you need to examine and analyze the clues that an author gives you about what he or she is feeling.

Determining the purpose of a text

When reading, the reader should always determine the purpose of a text. To do so, ask yourself what effect the writing has on you. Does the text try to explain or persuade you of something? Perhaps the text is making an appeal to your emotions. The signs that a text is attempting to persuade you include an author offering an opinion and explaining why she thinks this way. On the other hand, if a text is simply informative, it will have many facts that will give details about an event or person or a thing, but not try to persuade you of anything. Manuals that come with equipment are clearly not persuasive, simply instructive.

Explain the purpose of the passage below:

> Remember, no matter who you support, you have a duty as an American to voice your opinion on Tuesday. This is a privilege that so many people in other countries do not have, so make sure you get to your local polling place.

The purpose of the excerpt is to convince people to vote. This is clearly what the author wants to happen. He gives an argument for voting when he says it is your "duty as an American." He reasserts his purpose by telling people to "get to your local polling place." He uses reasons that he feels are important to urge people to vote, noting that many people in other countries do not have the same "privilege" of being able to vote for the candidate they choose. The author does not urge a particular person or party to vote for, simply that you should vote. This piece is meant to persuade.

Integrating information presented in different media or formats with words to develop a coherent understanding of a topic

When researching a topic or issue, you may find various ways that information is presented. It may be in written form, in a text; it may be in a visual form, including charts, lists or even videos. The way in which to come to an understanding of the information is to combine it as best as possible. While a text may have the larger picture about an issue, a chart could give you more specific information about one aspect of the issue at hand. A cartoon, for example, could give you a perspective that an informational report would not. Lists may help you categorize information about a topic and videos may give you a different perspective of the importance of an issue. Each representation has its place and it is important to use the benefit of the variety of presentations that exist to enhance your understanding of a topic.

Analyzing an argument

When reading a persuasive text, the first thing a reader should do is follow the way in which the author is building the argument. Look for the main contention that the author has and also the ways in which the author adds to her argument. Usually the author will include supporting information to her claims, but

- 139 -

that supporting information needs to be valid in order to support the claim. Look at the supporting evidence and notice where it comes from. Ask yourself if the evidence is based on facts and if the facts come from a reliable source or from a source that cannot be researched and confirmed. Be cautious of emotional claims that are based more on feelings than on fact. Throw out any claims that lack proper verification.

Read the excerpt and analyze the author's claim:

> We at Woodcrest Middle School should be more aware of our environment. We need to practice more recycling. It is important to our environment. According to an article written by ecologist Dr. Sam Schwartz, if every one of us recycled our school paper, we would see a 20 percent reduction in the waste at our school. So let's start today.

The author is claiming that recycling is important to the environment. He wants school students to recycle more. He uses supporting information from an article by ecologist Dr. Sam Schwartz. The fact that he has a doctorate degree is a good sign, but it would be better to find out where the article was published and a few more of his credentials as an expert. The author of the excerpt might have added these details to strengthen his claim. On the surface, however, the claim seems valid. The author does not use emotional appeals. The piece is quite straightforward and that is a good sign in such a text.

Memoir vs. biography

A memoir written by a person would include many intimate details about the person's feelings that a biographer might only guess at. The format would be much more personal than the format of a biography as well. The word *memoir* is French for "memory" and that is what a memoir is—the memories of an individual about his or her life. A biography would, by its very nature, be more formal than a memoir. A biographer is limited by the information he can research—and if the biographer is lucky enough to be able to interview the subject himself, the writer could add more personal details. Still, the biography would be written in the third person, which would give it more distance from the subject than a memoir would. On the other hand, a memoir can be very similar to an autobiography, which is written by the subject herself.

Importance of being a proficient reader of nonfiction texts

Being a proficient reader is essential to success at school and later in life, both in grade 6 and beyond. Comprehension of a wide range of nonfiction texts gives a student the ability to be at ease in reading schoolbooks and other texts throughout his life. Whether reading a science book, a newspaper, a railroad schedule or an instruction manual, a good reader will be able to interpret and find the information that is needed. Becoming a good reader involves reading a lot, looking up the meaning of words, and keeping word lists. This scaffolding will help improve the reading of any student and make him prepared for more difficult academic challenges.

Practice Test

Practice Questions

Questions 1 – 7 pertain to the following short story:

A World of White: The Iditarod Trail

(1) Imagine clinging desperately to your sled as brutal winds batter your body. The path ahead appears and disappears like a mirage, frequently obscured by blowing curtains of snow. You are freezing and sweating at the same time. Your throat burns with thirst, and your body aches with fatigue. You know your dogs must feel it too, so you encourage them to press on to the next checkpoint. All around you, the world is endless, empty, and white. Welcome to the Iditarod Trail.

(2) Alaska's Iditarod Trail is the world's most famous sled dog racing venue. But the trail is older than the sport of sled dog racing. In fact, the Iditarod Trail was first established in the early 1900s, during the Alaskan gold rush. In those days, dog teams were used for work, hauling thousands of pounds of gold from landlocked Iditarod to the port of Anchorage. But in faraway Nome, also known for gold, six-year-old George Allen had the idea to put together a race to see whose sled dogs were fastest, and the sport of sled dog racing was born.

(3) Though the Iditarod Trail race is the most famous race in the sport of sled dog racing, the first race along the trail was actually a race to save lives. In 1925, a diphtheria outbreak began in Nome. To prevent an epidemic that could kill thousands, doctors were desperate for the vaccine serum, but the closest serum was in Anchorage. The train ran from Anchorage to the village of Nenana, but that was still 674 miles from Nome. A cry for help was sent by the doctors, and in the midst of the blizzards and windstorms of January, the call was answered. Twenty brave mushers drove their dogs in a frantic relay, carrying 300,000 bottles of serum from Nenana to Nome. They followed the Iditarod Trail.

(4) Dog sledding, or "mushing," became quite popular after that heroic journey, but by the 1960s, it had lost popularity and the Iditarod Trail had been largely forgotten. There were a few lovers of mushing, however, who worked tirelessly to reestablish the Iditarod Trail and create a new sled dog race that used the trail as its course. The first official race was held in 1967 to celebrate the centennial of the purchase of Alaska from Russia. The race involved 58 drivers who mushed 56 miles in two days. This race was a success, but the popularity and future of the Iditarod Trail was still in question.

(5) In March of 1973, the first Anchorage to Nome Iditarod Trail race was organized and held. This race was much longer than previous races, covering more than 1,000 miles—the whole Iditarod Trail. Thirty-four mushers began the race, but only 22 were able to finish. After the 1973 race, the popularity of the Iditarod Trail finally grew and was firmly established. In 1978, the Iditarod Trail became a National Historic Trail.

(6) The modern Iditarod Trail race is open to mushers over 18 years old who have qualified in a recognized race of 200 miles or more. For younger mushers between 14 and 18 years old, the Junior Iditarod offers a 130-mile version of the race. Many Junior Iditarod participants go on to compete in the Iditarod Trail race, as the Junior Iditarod is good practice for the grueling trek of the main race. All mushers must prepare for the race

- 141 -

extensively, often for months before the race. Many mushers run their dogs more than 1,500 miles in preparation, giving them experience in all types of weather and terrain.

(7) To enter the Iditarod Trail race, participants must pay an entrance fee. Then they must travel to Anchorage with their dogs. In Anchorage, they attend a mushers' banquet where they are given their racing order numbers. Afterwards, all participating dogs are checked by a veterinarian and marked by race officials to prevent dog switching mid-race, which is not allowed. The dogs are even drug tested at the beginning and at checkpoints throughout the race to prevent cheating! Finally, the sleds and equipment are checked. Then participants are ready to start the race.

(8) On the morning of the Iditarod Trail race, mushers leave Anchorage in their assigned racing order. They are sent out one at a time, at two-minute intervals. For more than a week—sometimes up to three weeks—they travel throughout Alaska, stopping at designated checkpoints all along the Iditarod Trail as they make their way to Nome. When all participants have reached Nome, another mushers' banquet is held. Awards are given, and everyone is applauded for their achievement. Win or lose, the mushers know that only the toughest of the tough have what it takes to finish the race and conquer the great Iditarod Trail.

1. What does the simile in paragraph 1 describe?

    a. The snow
    b. The path
    c. The musher's throat
    d. The dogs

This question has two parts. Answer Part A then answer Part B.

2. Part A: What is the best description of the word "diphtheria" in paragraph 3?

    a. a mode of transportation
    b. an illness
    c. a trail name
    d. a celebration

Part B: Which sentence from the passage best supports your answer from Part A?

_____

_____

3. What is the author's main purpose in writing this article?

    a. To encourage mushers to race on the Iditarod Trail
    b. To inform the reader about the 1925 diphtheria outbreak
    c. To describe the terrain of Alaska
    d. To educate the reader about the Iditarod Trail

4. In paragraph 3, which words best convey the feelings of the doctors in Nome in 1925?

    a. "Epidemic" and "diphtheria"
    b. "Blizzards" and "windstorms"
    c. "Brave" and "frantic relay"
    d. "Desperate" and "cry for help"

5. Why did the author choose to write this article in third-person point of view?

    a. Historical overviews are best written in third person

    b. The author has never been to Alaska

    c. Third person is the required point of view in nonfiction writing

    d. This article is not written in third-person point of view

6. How is this article organized?

    a. Chronologically

    b. Geographically

    c. Randomly

    d. Spatially

This question has two parts. Answer Part A then answer Part B.

7. Part A: Which sentence is a main idea?

    a. To prevent an epidemic that could kill thousands, doctors were desperate for the vaccine serum, but the closest serum was in Anchorage.

    b. Alaska's Iditarod Trail is the world's most famous sled dog racing venue

    c. Thirty-four mushers began the race, but only 22 were able to finish.

    d. For more than a week—sometimes up to three weeks—they travel throughout Alaska, stopping at designated checkpoints all along the Iditarod Trail as they make their way to Nome.

Part B: Based on your answer in Part A. Which of the following is a supporting detail in this article?

    a. Alaska's Iditarod Trail is the world's most famous sled dog racing venue

    b. After the heroic journey of 1925, mushing became more popular

    c. In fact, the Iditarod Trail was first established in the early 1900s, during the Alaskan gold rush

    d. There are specific requirements to enter the Iditarod Trail race

Questions 8 –15 pertain to the following story:

The Right Thing to Do

Characters *(in order of appearance)*:

JESSICA—a sixth-grade girl, Amy's friend

GROUP OF FRIENDS—a group of sixth-grade girls

AMY—a sixth-grade girl, Jessica's friend

SALES CLERK—a clerk in the store Amy and Jessica visit

Scene 1

(1) *Jessica stands with a group of friends on the school steps. The group is chatting and laughing. Amy approaches from stage right.*

(2) AMY: Jessica! Jessica!

(3) JESSICA: *(turning away from her friends and taking a step toward Amy)* Hi, Amy. What's up?

(4) AMY: I'm headed to the mall, and I thought you might want to come.

- 143 -

(5) JESSICA: Why me? I thought we weren't friends anymore.

(6) AMY: *(waving her hand and shaking her head)* That old fight? Ancient history. So ... do you want to come or not?

(7) JESSICA: *(glancing back at her friends)* Sure. I'll come. Just give me a minute.

(8) *Jessica runs back and talks with her friends for a moment, then rejoins Amy. Amy and Jessica exit stage right.*

Scene 2

(9) *Amy and Jessica are looking at a shelf full of lipstick in a cosmetics store in the mall.*

(10) AMY: Look at this one, Jess. Don't you just love this color? *(She picks up a lipstick tube.)*

(11) JESSICA: It's nice, but I like this one better. *(She picks up a different tube of lipstick.)*

(12) *A sales clerk enters from stage left.*

(13) SALES CLERK: *(stopping by the girls)* Can I help you ladies find something?

(14) AMY: Oh, no. We're just looking.

(15) JESSICA: Thank you, though.

(16) SALES CLERK: Okay. Well, let me know if you need anything. *(He/she exits stage right.)*

(17) AMY: So, which one are you going to get?

(18) JESSICA: *(looking at the floor and shaking her head)* I'm not getting one. They're a little spendy for me. Besides, I'm saving up for something special.

(19) AMY: *(laughing)* Who said anything about money? *(She slips her favorite lipstick into her pocket.)* I didn't ask you which one you were going to buy. I asked which one you were going to get. So, which one will it be?

(20) JESSICA: But—but—that's stealing!

(21) AMY: Look at all these tubes of lipstick. They'll never miss a couple.

(22) JESSICA: *(looking around nervously)* What if that sales clerk comes back and catches us?

(23) AMY: You worry too much. *(She picks up two tubes of lipstick.)* Now, was this the one you liked? Or was it this one? Never mind. We'll take them both. *(She slips them both into her pocket.)*

(24) JESSICA: Amy! This is wrong. We shouldn't be doing this.

(25) AMY: *(glaring at Jessica)* Do you even want to be my friend again? It sure doesn't sound like it.

- 144 -

(26) JESSICA: Of course I want to be your friend. It's just—

(27) AMY: Then come on. Let's go. *(She starts to walk away, and then turns and looks back.)* Are you coming?

(28) JESSICA: Fine. *(She follows Amy.)* But what if the alarm goes off?

(29) AMY: For a couple of tubes of lipstick? Not gonna happen. Now, follow me. And for heaven's sake, don't look so nervous.

(30) *The girls exit stage right.*

Scene 3

(31) *Jessica reenters the cosmetics store from stage right. She stops at the shelf of lipsticks and looks around. The sales clerk enters from stage left.*

(32) JESSICA: Excuse me …

(33) SALES CLERK: *(stopping)* Did you need help with something?

(34) JESSICA: Yes. *(She looks at the floor.)* My friend who was just with me, um, she took— well, actually, she stole three tubes of lipstick. I'm not okay with that. So, um, I wanted to pay for them.

(35) SALES CLERK: That's impressive. I've never seen that happen before. And kids take stuff from this store all the time. What made you come back?

(36) JESSICA: *(shrugging)* I don't know. I guess it was just the right thing to do.

This question has two parts. Answer Part A then answer Part B.

8. Part A: In paragraph 6, what does Amy mean when she calls her fight with Jessica "ancient history"?
    a. It happened thousands of years ago
    b. It happened in history class
    c. Amy has totally forgotten about the fight
    d. They were arguing about events in ancient history

Part B: Which sentence supports your answer from Part A?
    a. That old fight?
    b. Sure. I'll come.
    c. I'm headed to the mall, and I thought you might want to come.
    d. *Jessica runs back and talks with her friends for a moment, then rejoins Amy.*

9. What is the setting for Scene 1?
    a. The school steps
    b. The mall
    c. A cosmetics store
    d. Amy's house

10. What is the setting for Scene 2 and Scene 3?

    a. The school steps
    b. Jessica's house
    c. A cosmetics store
    d. Amy's house

11. Which scene contains the climax of this play?

    a. Scene 1
    b. Scene 2
    c. Scene 3
    d. All of the above

12. Which scene contains the denouement of this play?

    a. Scene 1
    b. Scene 2
    c. Scene 3
    d. All of the above

13. In paragraph 6, what type of figurative language is used when Amy says "ancient history"?

    a. Metaphor
    b. Simile
    c. Personification
    d. Hyperbole

14. What is the underlying theme of this play?.

    a. Amy and Jessica are best friends
    b. Doing the right thing is always a good decision
    c. It is okay to steal if you are not caught
    d. Shopping for cosmetics increases peer pressure

15. Which paragraph best shows Amy's justification for stealing the lipstick?

    a. Paragraph 21
    b. Paragraph 23
    c. Paragraph 25
    d. Paragraph 29

Questions 16– 25 pertain to the following two short stories:

The Talent Show

(1) The first notes floated from the piano. Megan smiled, warm and excited beneath the glaring stage lights. This was her moment. She had practiced. She had prepared. She was ready. As the introduction ended, Megan opened her mouth and began to sing.

(2) The song flowed along, and Megan relaxed, scanning the faces of the audience. But somewhere in the middle of the second verse, her mind suddenly went blank. The music went on, but the words were gone. Megan's smile faded. She stood silently with her mouth hanging open. When the music finally trickled to a stop, Megan ran from the stage.

(3) In a cramped dressing room backstage, Megan buried her face in her hands. She had wanted so much to win this talent show. Tears seeped between her fingers. Her

- 146 -

confidence and pride and excitement had been replaced by utter disappointment. She felt a hand on her shoulder and lifted her damp face.

(4) "Ella and Kaylee are here," Megan's mom said, giving her shoulder a quick squeeze.

(5) Ella and Kaylee, Megan's two best friends, pulled folding chairs over to face Megan. She looked at them forlornly.

(6) "I'm a total failure," she moaned.

(7) Ella and Kaylee exchanged glances. Kaylee reached out and squeezed Megan's hand.

(8) "What are you talking about?" Kaylee said. "That first verse was some of your best singing ever."

(9) "Thanks," Megan said. "But the problem is that the first verse is all I sang. Then I totally bombed. I can't believe I forgot the words after all that practice."

(10) "You didn't totally bomb," Ella said. "You just forgot the words. That happens to everybody. Besides, don't the pros say you should leave your audience wanting more?"

(11) "I guess so," Megan admitted.

(12) "Well, trust me," Ella said. "I guarantee they wanted more—like the rest of the song! You probably did, too."

(13) Megan smiled a little. "So, you guys don't think I'm a total dork for forgetting the words?"

(14) "Of course not," Kaylee said. "Forgetting the words doesn't make you a dork. It just makes you human. And you're still the most talented person I know."

(15) Ella nodded in agreement. Megan pulled Ella and Kaylee into a quick hug. Then she wiped her eyes and managed a genuine smile.

(16) "I'm so lucky to have best friends like you two," Megan said. "It's nice to know that you'll be my friends forever, no matter what!"

The Tournament

(1) Looking for a hole in the defense, Scott dribbled the ball, shifting it from hand to hand. A trickle of sweat ran down his back. No one was open. There were only seconds left on the clock, and Scott knew he had a difficult decision to make.

(2) The other team was leading by two points, and Scott was just outside the three-point line. If he could make the shot, the Eagles would be state champions again. But if he missed … Scott didn't want to think about that. He knew what he had to do.

(3) It was a classic jump shot. The ball left his hands and sailed toward the basket in a perfect arc. The crowd, the other players, the whole stadium seemed frozen in time. All

- 147 -

eyes were on the ball as it struck the rim and bounced off. The buzzer blared. The game was over. Scott had missed, and the Eagles had lost.

(4) Scott stood like a statue on the court as people surged around him. Elated family members swarmed the winning team. Teammates hugged and slapped each other on the back. Even Scott's own teammates joined in the celebration.

(5) Suddenly, Scott felt himself being hoisted unsteadily onto the shoulders of his friends. Over the loudspeaker, the announcer proclaimed that Scott had been named the most valuable player of the championship game. Everyone cheered, and the Eagles took a victory lap with Scott on their shoulders. Finally, Scott's friends put him back on solid ground.

(6) Scott was bewildered. He was the one who missed the most important shot of the game. How could anyone call him the most valuable player? He didn't feel very valuable at the moment. Scott approached Coach Travis.

(7) "Coach," Scott said, "there must be some mistake. I can't be the most valuable player."

(8) "There's no mistake," Coach Travis said. "You had 26 points, 11 rebounds, and 8 assists. I'd say that makes you a very valuable player."

(9) "But I missed that last shot," Scott said. "We lost the game because of me."

(10) "I don't know about that," said Coach Travis. "Everybody misses a shot from time to time. Don't be so hard on yourself. It's all about perspective."

(11) "What do you mean?" Scott asked.

(12) "Well," Coach Travis answered, "you could say you are the reason we lost the game because you missed that last shot. On the other hand, you could say you are the reason we almost won because of your awesome performance throughout the game. How you look at it is up to you."

(13) Scott's teammates came running over and surrounded Coach Travis. They jostled one another playfully, talking and laughing.

(14) "Hey, Coach," one player called out, "how about treating your team to pizza?"

(15) "I don't know," said Coach Travis. "Do you think you deserve pizza?"

(16) Scott piped up. "Of course we do! After all, we almost won the game."

(17) Coach Travis smiled. "You're right, Scott. We did almost win. Okay. Pizza for everyone!"

Questions 16-20 pertain to "The Talent Show" short story:

16. Which of the following is the best definition of "forlornly" as it is used in paragraph 5?
    a. With a happy spirit
    b. With a sad spirit
    c. With a lonely spirit
    d. With an angry spirit

- 148 -

17. What is the main theme of this story?

    a. Real friends support you, no matter what
    b. It is easy to forget the words of a song
    c. Performing in a talent show can be embarrassing
    d. Megan feels like a failure

18. Which of the following is a supporting detail in this story?

    a. Megan is singing in a talent show
    b. Megan forgets the words of her song
    c. Megan is disappointed in herself
    d. Megan is accompanied by piano music

19. What does Kaylee do in paragraph 8 to try to make Megan feel better?

    a. She makes a joke about Megan's performance
    b. She compliments Megan on her singing
    c. She tells about a time when she forgot a song
    d. She sings a song with Megan

Questions 21-25 pertain to "The Tournament" short story:

20. In paragraph 4, what does "elated" mean?

    a. Happy and excited
    b. Frustrated and angry
    c. Loud and rowdy
    d. Pushy and proud

21. In the first sentence of paragraph 4, what type of figurative language is used?

    a. Hyperbole
    b. Metaphor
    c. Personification
    d. Simile

22. Which of the following is the best summary of this story?

    a. At the buzzer, Scott misses an important basket because he isn't a very good basketball player
    b. Coach Travis feels Scott is the most valuable player in the game because he scored 26 points
    c. When Scott misses an important shot, he is disappointed, but Coach Travis shows him there are different ways to look at the situation
    d. The Eagles lose the state championship because of Scott, but Coach Travis sees things differently and makes Scott the most valuable player

23. Why is Scott so upset in this story?

    a. He feels responsible for losing the game
    b. He thinks he is a bad basketball player
    c. He doesn't like Coach Travis
    d. He doesn't want to play basketball anymore

Questions 24-25 pertain to both "The Talent Show" and "The Tournament" short stories:

24. In what ways are Scott and Megan most similar in these stories?

   a. They are both performers.
   b. They are both very active.
   c. They are both disappointed in themselves.
   d. They both have good friends.

This question has two parts. Answer Part A then answer Part B.

25. Part A: What general theme is evident in both stories?

   a. Winning is important, but it isn't everything
   b. Good friends are the most valuable thing in life
   c. Coaches can offer good perspective on tough situations
   d. When you try your best, you shouldn't be disappointed in yourself

Part B: Write down a sentence or sentences from each story that proves this is true.

_____

_____

_____

_____

_____

Questions 26-29 pertain to the following story:

Everybody's Problem

(1) I used to think homeless people were dirty and lazy and mean. I thought they were all old men with scraggly beards and mangy dogs. I thought they lived on the street because they wanted to. I thought they were all drug addicts and alcoholics who ate from garbage cans and slept in boxes. I used to think homelessness wasn't my problem. Then I met Chris, and he showed me I was wrong—about everything. Homelessness is everybody's problem.

(2) The sun was climbing into the bright blue sky as we loaded up the bus at the youth center. It was a crisp, cold Thanksgiving morning, and our youth group was headed down to a local shelter called The Lighthouse. We were going to serve Thanksgiving dinner to more than a hundred homeless people. It seemed like an appropriate way to spend Thanksgiving Day.

(3) When we arrived at the shelter, we were each given a job to do. My job was peeling potatoes. The shelter director gave me a peeler and a garbage can and sat me down in front of a giant pile of potatoes. I had never seen so many potatoes in one place before. They rose from the tray like Mt. Everest. By the time I had peeled them all, my hands and arms and shoulders ached.

(4) When the kitchen work was done, we were given our serving stations. The director explained that this was the only meal many of the homeless people would eat that day, and for some, it was the only hot meal they would have that week. Even so, there wasn't a lot of

- 150 -

food for so many people. We were supposed to give each person one slice of turkey, one scoop of mashed potatoes, one scoop of stuffing, a small drizzle of gravy, a few green beans, and a sliver of pumpkin pie.

(5) I was plodding along, dishing up mashed potatoes with an ice cream scoop, when I happened to look up at the person I was serving. He wasn't a dirty, bearded old man. He was a boy about my age, with brown hair and brown eyes and a patched green jacket.

(6) "Hi," the boy said. "I'm Chris."

(7) "I'm Ben," I said as I scooped some potatoes onto his plate. "Happy Thanksgiving."

(8) "Thanks," Chris said, and then he was gone.

(9) As Chris moved down the line, I began to look around, really seeing things for the first time. Very few of the homeless people fit my stereotype. There were men and women, old and young. Children played in a corner of the dining room. At one table, teenagers talked in a tight group. People chatted and smiled. A few were even laughing. This was not what I had pictured a homeless shelter would be like.

(10) When everyone had been served, I began to help clean up. I couldn't help watching Chris as I cleared the tables and wiped them down. He was playing peek-a-boo with a little girl in a high chair. I wondered if it was his little sister.

(11) I was so lost in thought that I jumped when the shelter director tapped my shoulder. She laughed.

(12) "I'll finish cleaning up here," she said. "Why don't you go talk to Chris? He's very nice."

(13) As I approached the table where Chris was sitting, I felt nervous. What would I say? Could we possibly have anything to talk about? Would he even want to talk to me? I sat cautiously beside him.

(14) "Hi, Ben," he said.

(15) "Hi, Chris. Is that your little sister?"

(16) Chris smiled. "Yep. This is Sophia. And over there is my little brother, Dane." Chris motioned toward the corner where the smaller children were playing. Then he pointed to a dark-haired woman at a nearby table. "That's my mom."

(17) "Are you all homeless?" I asked.

(18) "Yep," answered Chris. "We've been here at The Lighthouse for almost two months now. It's okay here, but I miss my old school and my friends. I hope we can move back to a real house soon."

(19) "I didn't know there was such a thing as homeless kids," I admitted.

(20) "Me neither," said Chris. "At least, not until I became one."

(21) "How did it happen?" I asked. Then I had second thoughts. "I mean, you don't have to tell me if you don't want to. I was just wondering."

(22) "It's okay," Chris said. "I don't mind talking about it. About a year ago, my dad got really sick. He was in the hospital for a few months. Then he died. We didn't have any insurance or anything, and my mom couldn't get a job. Besides, she was really sad, and she was trying to take care of me and Dane and Sophia."

(23) "So, how did you end up homeless?" I wondered.

(24) "Mom says there were just too many bills and not enough money. First, we got our lights turned off. Then we couldn't pay our rent, so we had to move out of our house. We stayed with friends for a while, but eventually there was nobody left to stay with. So, we came here."

(25) "Will you stay here forever?" I asked.

(26) "No," Chris said. "My mom is in a program to give her training and help her get a job. When she finds a job, we can get a new place to live. Then things can be normal again."

(27) i heard my youth leader calling for us to load the bus. I wanted to talk to Chris more and ask him more questions, but I knew I had to leave. I stood up.

(28) "I have to go," I said. "I'm glad I got to meet you, Chris. I hope you get a new house soon."

(29) "Thanks, Ben," Chris said. "It was nice to meet you, too. Thanks for hanging out with me for a while. Happy Thanksgiving."

(30) "Happy Thanksgiving," I echoed as I headed toward the door. When I looked back, Chris waved. Then he started playing peek-a-boo with Sophia again.

(31) I will probably never see Chris again, but I have thought of him many times since that day. In just a few minutes together, he taught me so much about the problem of homelessness. It isn't just a problem that affects lazy, mean old men. It affects men and women of all ages. It affects children. It affects whole families. It affected Chris. And because I got the chance to see homelessness through his eyes, it affects me now, too. I think I'll go back again next Thanksgiving ... or maybe sooner. After all, now I know that homelessness is everybody's problem.

26. What is the setting for this story?
    a. A youth center
    b. A homeless shelter
    c. A community center
    d. A school

27. If you were describing this story, what classification would you use?
    a. Memoir
    b. Biography
    c. Autobiography
    d. Fiction

28. In paragraph 9, what does the word "stereotype" mean?
   a. A textbook definition of a concept
   b. Height, weight, and physical features
   c. A generalized idea of what something is like
   d. A description given by an authority figure

29. What point of view is used to tell this story?
   a. First person
   b. Second person
   c. Third person
   d. All of the above

Answers and Explanations

1. B: A simile compares one thing to another by using "like" or "as"; the only simile in paragraph 1—"like a mirage"—refers to the path.

2. Part A: B: "Diphtheria" is a type of respiratory illness.
Part B: This sentence best supports the answer from Part A: "To prevent an epidemic that could kill thousands, doctors were desperate for the vaccine serum, but the closest serum was in Anchorage." It talks about needing a vaccine which is used to cure illnesses.

3. D: This is an informational article – the author's main purpose in writing this article is to educate the reader about the Iditarod Trail.

4. D: The descriptive word "desperate" and the descriptive phrase "cry for help" are used in reference to the doctors in Nome in 1925.

5. A: Historical overviews, like this one, are best written in the third-person point of view.

6. A: This article is organized chronologically, from earliest to latest dates.

7. Part A: B: This is the only sentence that gives a main idea. All of the other choices are just supporting details.
Part B: C: is a supporting detail that expands on a main idea from the article. A, B, and D are not the best choices because they are all main points in the article instead of supporting details.

8. Part A: C: The phrase "ancient history" is a figure of speech. Amy uses it to communicate that she has totally forgotten about the fight.
Part B: A: Amy refers to it as "that old fight", which shows that it happened a while back and she has already forgotten about it.

9. A: Scene 1 is set on the school steps.

10. C: Scene 2 and Scene 3 take place in a cosmetics store.

11. B: Scene 2 contains the climax of the play, when Jessica must decide whether to go along with Amy or not. In a story, the climax is the most exciting part of the story, when the action or tension builds to a zenith. This occurred when Jessica learned that Amy was planning on stealing the lipstick.

12. C: Scene 3 contains the denouement of the play, when Jessica returns to the store to do the right thing. This is also known as the resolution of the story.

13. D: The use of "ancient history" in paragraph 6 is a hyperbole, a major exaggeration.

14. B: The underlying theme of the play is that you should always do the right thing, even when it's difficult. This could also be called the moral of the story.

15. A: In Paragraph 21, Amy tries to justify stealing the tubes of lipstick by saying that the store has a lot of them, and stealing only two or three of them won't do any harm because they won't even be missed.

16. B: "Forlornly" is best defined as "with a sad spirit."

17. A most accurately represents the main theme of the story.

18. D: is only option that offers a supporting detail, while the rest of the answer choices represent important parts of the story.

19. B: In paragraph 8, Kaylee compliments Megan's singing to help her feel better.

20. A: If someone is "elated", they are extremely happy and excited about something.

21. D: The first sentence of paragraph 4 uses a simile when it says Scott "stood like a statue." A simile uses "like" or "as" to compare one thing to another.

22. C is the most complete and accurate summary of the story overall. A, B, and D are incorrect because they cover only part of the story or some of the main ideas and concepts.

23. A: Scott is upset in the story because he feels responsible for the team's loss.

24. C: Scott and Megan are most similar in their feelings of disappointment in themselves.

25. Part A: D: clearly reflects a general theme found in both stories.

Part B: An example from *The Talent Show* is, "Forgetting the words doesn't make you a dork. It just makes you human. And you're still the most talented person I know." An example from *The Tournament* is, "Well," Coach Travis answered, "you could say you are the reason we lost the game because you missed that last shot. On the other hand, you could say you are the reason we almost won because of your awesome performance throughout the game. How you look at it is up to you."

26. B: This story is set at a homeless shelter.

27. A: This story is written in the style of a memoir, as evidenced by the first-person, reflective tone.

28. C offers the best definition of "stereotype" as it is used in paragraph 9.

29. A: This story is written in first person. That means the author is involved in the events of the story and is telling it from his point of view.

English

Pronouns

Pronouns can be subjective, objective or possessive. A *subjective pronoun* is a pronoun that takes the place of the noun that is the subject of a sentence. For example, in the sentence "They went for a trip to the country," the pronoun "they" is in the subjective pronoun. Other subjective pronouns are "I," "it," "you," "he," "she," and "we." An *objective pronoun* takes the place of the noun that is the predicate of a sentence. For example, in the sentence "Tom threw the baseball to him," the objective pronoun is "him." Other objective pronouns are "me," "it," "you," "her," "us," and "them." *Possessive pronouns* take the place of possessive nouns. In the sentence "Their coats were warm," The possessive pronoun is "their." Other possessive pronouns are "my," "mine," "his," "hers," "ours," and "yours."

Identify the errors in the following sentence and correct them:

Me and Billy are going to the football game with him brother.

There are two errors in pronoun usage in the sentence. The first one is the incorrect choice of an objective pronoun as a subject of the sentence. The "me" should be "I." This is the proper choice of pronoun for first person singular. Also, the placement of the pronoun is incorrect. It should follow the other part of the compound subject and read "Billy and I." The "him" before the word "brother" is also incorrect. This should be a possessive pronoun, but "him" is an objective pronoun. It is supposed to be the possessive pronoun "his." The revised sentence should read: "Billy and I are going to the football game with his brother."

Intensive pronouns are used to emphasize another pronoun or noun. They are formed by putting "self" after objective pronouns, such as "myself," "yourself," "herself," "himself," "itself," "ourselves," "yourselves" and "themselves." For example, the following sentence uses an intensive pronoun for emphasis: "Desiree is going to lead the parade herself." When these pronouns are used on their own they are called *reflexive pronouns*; a reflexive pronoun refers to a noun or another pronoun and indicates that the same person or thing is involved. For example, the sentence "We bought this hockey equipment ourselves" contains the reflexive pronoun "ourselves."

Identify the errors in the following sentence and correct them:

Shirley, itself, will take care of finding a new place to practice.

This sentence contains an error in the use of the intensive pronoun. An intensive pronoun must agree with the noun that it is modifying. In this case, the intensive pronoun must agree with "Shirley," but "itself" refers to an object or thing and not a person. The correct pronoun form would be "herself" because it is a female-gender singular pronoun. So the sentence should read: "Shirley, herself, will take care of finding a new place to practice." In the sentence, the pronoun is used to create a sense of emphasis. This pronoun usage is different from a reflexive pronoun. Instead of emphasizing a noun or pronoun, a reflexive pronoun refers back to a noun or pronoun.

Identify the errors in the following sentence and correct them:

Tennis is thought to have their origins in the Orient.

This sentence contains an incorrect possessive pronoun. While "their" is supposed to refer to "tennis" as its antecedent, it does not agree with that noun either in number or person. Tennis is the name of a game. It is not a person, so the use of the pronoun "their" is incorrect because it refers to people. Tennis is also a singular noun so it does not agree with the plural possessive pronoun "their." The sentence needs to be

- 155 -

corrected so that the possessive pronoun is singular and agrees with the noun "tennis." The correct possessive pronoun is "its." The revised sentence should read, "Tennis is thought to have its origins in the Orient."

Rewrite the following sentence to make it clearer what the pronoun "it" refers to:

> If you leave your notebook in your backpack, you will forget it.

What does the sentence mean? It is unclear in the sentence whether "it" refers to "notebook" or "backpack." The sentence could be interpreted in either way. The problem is that there is no clear antecedent, so the sentence must be rewritten to make the writer's intention evident. The best way to write the sentence to correct the error is, "You will forget your notebook if you leave it in your backpack." That way, "it" clearly refers to "notebook" and not "backpack," making the meaning of the sentence obvious. When you write, make sure that all pronouns clearly refer to the noun or pronoun intended. They should also agree in number and person.

Identify the errors in the following sentences and correct them:

> Many who learn the trombone may have his difficulties at first. Each of the musical instruments presents their own challenge.

Both sentences contain an incorrect pronoun. In the first sentence, the possessive pronoun "his" does not agree with the plural indefinite pronoun "many." "Many" takes a plural possessive form, so the first sentence should read, "Many who learn the trombone may have *their* difficulties." The second sentence has the opposite problem: the indefinite pronoun "each" is singular, so the pronoun that refers to it must be singular as well. The correct possessive form of "each" is "its" because the sentence is talking about a thing and not a person. So the correct way to write the second sentence is, "Each of the musical instruments presents its own challenge." The second sentence is tricky because the plural noun "instruments" might be interpreted as the antecedent, but it is not. "Each" is the subject of the sentence and the antecedent for "its."

Commas, parentheses, and dashes

Commas, parentheses, and dashes are used to set off nonrestrictive or parenthetical elements in a sentence. They are used to keep the extra information apart from the flow of the sentence. In the following sentence, commas are used to set aside additional information: "The word tycoon comes from a Japanese word, *taikun*, meaning mighty lord, which in turn comes from two Chinese words." In this next sentence, the additional information is set apart by parentheses: "The ruins of ancient Troy are located in Turkey, about four miles (6.4 kilometers) from the mouth of the Dardanelles." Here, parentheses are used to set off the additional information that the writer wanted to include without making it a formal part of the sentence. Generally, it is best to use parentheses when including dates or data about someone or something. Finally, dashes are used in the following sentence to set information apart: "The circus performer was sitting calmly in a chair—fifty feet above the crowd—while waving a flag."

Identify the errors in the following sentences and correct them:

> Most people do not know that the sandwich was named after John Montagu, the fourth Earl of Sandwich 1718-1782.

> During the reign of Elizabeth I, England by defeating the Spanish Armada in 1588 became a great sea power.

The best way to separate the extra information in the first sentence from the rest of the sentence is by using parentheses, which are commonly used to separate dates or data. This would make the sentence

- 156 -

both clearer and grammatically correct, which it is not at the present moment. The sentence should read: "Most people do not know that the sandwich was named after John Montagu, the fourth Earl of Sandwich (1718-1782)." Be sure to put the period after the closing parenthesis and not before it. The second sentence has information that is an aside, and needs to be separated from the main sentence. Either commas or dashes would work. So the sentence could be written: "During the reign of Elizabeth I, England, by defeating the Spanish Armada in 1588, became a great sea power." Or it could be: "During the reign of Elizabeth I, England—by defeating the Spanish Armada in 1588—became a great sea power.

Which words are misspelled in the following sentence?
    She hoped that the lectore would benifit her understanding of fine litarature.

The words that are misspelled are "lectore," "benifit," and "litarature," which are spelled "lecture," "benefit," and "literature" respectively. It is important to learn to spell words correctly. There are certain skills you can use to help you spell words correctly. Sounding out words is one of them. Breaking longer words down into syllables, affixes, and roots can help you figure out the way a word should be spelled. Making a list of new words is a good habit to get into, and using those words in sentences will help you remember them. Also, use the basic spelling rules, such as "I before E except after C," (believe) as well as "drop the final e" (take, taking) and "double the last consonant" (hop, hopping).

Context clues

Context clues are the clues that are contained in the sentence or sentences around an unknown word. A reader can often figure out the meaning of an unknown word from these clues. For instance, a passage might say that John and Stan had absolute trust in each other's decisions. A reader might not be familiar with the word "absolute," but then the passage goes on to say that John and Stan really believed in each other and always accepted each other's decisions. These facts give clues about the meaning of "absolute." The reader could conclude that "absolute" means "total" or "complete." Another helpful clue is that the word "absolute" comes before a noun, "trust," so it is logical to think that it is an adjective. This tells the reader that the word and any synonyms for it must also be adjectives.

Using context clues, determine the meaning of "specializes" in the following excerpt:
    Charley is a great salesman. He can sell books and beds and towels and washing machines.
    He can sell anything. But Charley specializes in selling carpets. That is all he sells now.

You can figure out from the excerpt that the word "specializes" means "concentrates"—doing one thing. The context clues tell you this is the word's meaning. The excerpt says that Charley is a great salesman and that he can sell books, beds, towels and washing machines. In fact, the excerpt says he can sell anything, but it ends by saying that he only sells carpets now—he *specializes* in that. If you substitute the words "concentrates on" for "specializes in," the sentence makes sense. He is only selling carpets now. Both words are verbs, so that helps to let you know that this is probably the correct choice of synonym.

Affixes and roots

A *root word* is a word that can be added onto. An *affix* is a prefix or suffix that is added onto a root word. Often, the affixes in the English language come from Latin or Greek origins. A *prefix* is added to the beginning of a root word and a *suffix* is added to the end of a root word. When you look at the meaning of a root word and the meaning of any affixes added to the root word, you can figure out the approximate meaning of the word. For example, the root word "happy" means "to be content." The prefix "un-" means "not." The reader can therefore figure out that "unhappy" means to "not being content."

<u>Figuring out the meaning of the word "misconception" based on its root and affixes</u>

The word "misconception" is made up of three sections: a root, a prefix, and a suffix. To figure out the meaning of the word, you need to analyze these parts of the word individually. The root "concept" means "idea." It comes from the Latin word *conceptus* meaning "something conceived. There are two affixes in the word. The prefix *mis-* means "not" or "bad." The suffix *-tion* means "action" or "process." Put these meanings together and the word "misconception" means "the act of having a bad idea" or "misunderstanding." Studying roots and affixes is important because it allows you to decode words that you might not otherwise understand with relative ease.

Using specialized reference materials to determine the pronunciation of a word

A print or digital dictionary can be used as a means to find the correct pronunciation of words. The dictionary will have a guide that shows how to sound out the words, the symbols used to indicate the sounds, along with sample sounds (like the "i" in "pie," for instance). The dictionary can also be used to determine the meaning of the word, as well as its part of speech. The thesaurus is useful because it lists synonyms for all the various meanings a word can have, which helps to clarify the precise meaning as used in the context of the text you are reading. Many books will have a glossary placed at the end of the book to help you with difficult or unfamiliar words used in the text.

Julia used her dictionary to check the various meanings of the word "clear." She found this entry:

clear (klîr) adj. 1.obvious. 2. easily seen through. 3. free from flaw or blemish. 4. free from guilt; untroubled 5. out of the way. v. int. 6. to tidy. 7. to free 8. To earn.

Identify which definition of "clear" is used in the following sentence:

Janet stood clear of the crowd pushing to get through the door.

The correct answer is meaning 5: "out of the way." If you substitute that definition for the word, the sentence makes sense. Meanings 1, 2, 3, and 4 do not fit with the context of the sentence. Meanings 6, 7, and 8 are verbs and "clear" as it is used in the sample is an adjective. When considering which meaning is being used, always check for context clues in the sentence or in the sentences before or after the sentence in which the word is used. Dictionaries also tell you how to pronounce words and often the derivation of the word, although that is not given here.

Discuss the meaning of the word "steep" in the following sentence:

The price of the designer shoes was too steep for Stephanie to even consider buying them.

The word "steep" can mean many things. In this instance, it means "expensive." The context of the sentence helps the reader figure this out because the sentence says that Stephanie would not even consider buying the shoes because the price was too "steep." If you substitute the word "expensive" for "steep," the sentence continues to make sense. This is a good way to determine if you have the correct meaning of a word. The other meanings of the word "steep" do not fit in the sentence. To figure out the meaning of the word, use the context clues and then check the meaning of the word in a dictionary. A dictionary will also help determine the meaning of the word by saying what part of speech it is when used in a particular instance. In this case the word "steep" is used as an adjective.

Explain what figure of speech is used in the following sentence:

The wind called out to the lost pioneers, warning them to take shelter.

This is an example of personification, one of many different figures of speech. *Personification* is the act of giving human traits to things. Here the wind is "calling out" and "warning" the pioneers. Wind does not really call out or warn people. It may seem as though it does, but only people can call out or warn people. Other kinds of figures of speech or figurative language include *similes*, which uses the words "like" and "as" to compare two things to each other; *metaphors*, where two things are compared without using comparison words; and *hyperbole*, an exaggeration meant to create an impression without being taken literally.

Using the relationships between words to better understand them

You can use the relationships between words to better understand them. Some words indicate a cause and effect relationship. These include "as a result," "because," "since" and "consequently," to name a few. When you see these words, you will know that a cause and effect relationship exists, which may help you understand how the words relate to one another. Other relationship words include "part" and "whole" and "item" and "category." A whole is made up of parts, and a category is made up of items. If you see the word "part," look for the word that is the whole. If you see the word "item," look for the word that is the category. In this way you will better understand these terms.

Connotations vs. denotations of words

The *denotation* of a word is what the dictionary definition of that word is. The *connotation* of a word is what the word suggests beyond its dictionary meaning. It is both the meaning that is associated with that word and a subjective interpretation of the word's meaning. The denotation meaning is objective. For instance, the words "stingy" and "thrifty" basically mean not being wasteful. However, "stingy" carries with it the connotation of being thrifty to such an extent as to be seen as being miserly; it is not a positive term. "Thrifty" can be seen as a virtue, while "stingy" is not. When you read, you should pay particular attention to the language that a writer uses to describe something. Look for words that suggest something about a place or person that are not directly stated in the text.

Determine the difference in the connotations between the words "doting" and "affectionate."
The word "doting" is a term that is used to convey a negative connotation in that it means caring about someone excessively, to the point of overlooking the reality of the person. "Affectionate," on the other hand, has a more positive connotation of someone who simply cares for someone else very much. "Doting" is a much more extreme word. It suggests a lot about a person who is described as doting, as though the person would overlook any wrongdoing by the person that is being cared for. "Affectionate" does not have that extreme meaning; it is more benign.

Improving comprehension

It is important to acquire and accurately use words and phrases at the appropriate level so as to improve comprehension and expression. Such a skill helps the student to perform well in the classroom as well as on standardized testing. A student who does not read at the appropriate level will have to continually stop while reading so he or she can look up the meaning of words. Someone who does not have a good vocabulary will take a great deal longer to comprehend new material in class as well as information that may be encountered in life. Students should make an attempt to develop their vocabulary by keeping lists of new words and using them in sentences. Students should be very familiar with dictionary use as well as thesaurus use. Having a good vocabulary is valuable not only for reading well, but also for writing well. It is important, too, to be able to express what you mean precisely and for that you need to improve your vocabulary.

Practice Test

Practice Questions

Questions 1 – 9 pertain to the following article:

The Trouble with Tests

(1) Lisa was a good student. (2) She studied hard, diligently did her homework, and turned in assignments on time. (3) Whenever she had to take a test, however, Lisa had a problem. (4) Her hands began to sweat and her stomach began to churn. (5) She felt dizzy breathless and sick. (6) As a result, Lisa couldn't focus and always did poorly on tests. (7) Her grades suffered, and so did her confidence level.

(8) Lisa's problem is a common one. (9) Often called test anxiety, it includes any unusual stress symptoms that occur during tests. (10) Symptoms can be as mild as light nausea or headache, or as severe as vomiting or uncontrollable shaking. (11) Millions of students deal with test anxiety every year, but few realize it can be improved through three simple steps.

(12) The first step to improving test anxiety is better study habits. (13) Proper preparation is an important step to overcoming test anxiety. (14) It is important to develop regular study times avoiding last minute "cramming" for a test. (15) Studying heavily on the day of or night before a test can actually increase test anxiety in most students. (16) The better option is to devote at least a half-hour block of time to review class materials each day. (17) This can help embedding information in the brain, making it more accessible at test time.

(18) Using memory games and tools is another way to improve study habits. (19) Using these tools and games can help students better retain information. (20) It also makes learning more fun, by reducing stress levels. (21) Flashcards with key points or ideas can be very helpful when used alone or with a study partner. (22) Mnemonic devices—silly sayings to help students recall complex concepts—are also helpful tools for reducing stress and improving test performance. (23) An example of a mnemonic device is "Every Good Boy Deserves Fudge" to help music students remember the note names for the lines of the treble clef staff (EGBDF).

(24) The second step to reducing test anxiety is to use relaxation techniques. (25) The first relaxation technique that is useful for test anxiety is visualization. (26) This involves choosing a favorite place or event. (27) When test anxiety symptoms appear, students can close there eyes and visualize themselves in that favorite place or at that favorite event. (28) The students should focus on sensory information—sights, sounds, smells, etc. (29) This refocuses the attention of the brain and reduces anxiety.

(30) Another relaxation technique that works well for test anxiety is deep breathing. (31) When the body is under stress, breathing becomes shallower, causing the heart rate to increase and the blood pressure to rise. (32) Conscious deep breathing helps increase oxygen flow to the body, reducing the heart rate and blood pressure. (33) To do deep breathing, simply draw air in through the nose for five seconds, and then release the air through the mouth, blowing out steadily for five seconds. (34) Done with eyes open or closed, deep breathing exercises reduce stress and relax the body.

(35) The third step to reducing test anxiety is positive self-talk. (36) Often, test anxiety is the result of or is compounded by a lack of faith in abilities. (37) Students can overcome this through positive self-talk and self-affirmation. (38) Before each test, a student should repeat, "I can do this"—or some similar positive mantra—over and over. (39) This can be done out loud or silently; either way, it creates a positive attitude and outlook, that can reduce anxiety.

(40) The self-affirmation of celebrating success is a final key to overcoming test anxiety. (41) Students should share test-taking victories with friends and loved ones. (42) Students should also feel proud when they do well on a test. (43) Every success is a blow to the obstacle of test anxiety. (44) As with anything else, practice makes perfect, and celebrating success helps a student practice triumph over test anxiety.

(45) Test anxiety is a real problem, not an imagined issue or an excuse. (46) It can be overcome, however, through three basic steps. (47) First, students must use study tools and good habits for proper preparation. (48) Second, students must use relaxation techniques—such as visualization and deep breathing—to help release stress from the body. (49) Finally, students must engage in positive selftalk and celebrate successes to create an atmosphere of triumph. (50) When all three of these steps are consistently practiced, test anxiety will become a thing of the past.

1. What change, if any, should be made to sentence 5?

    a. No change
    b. She felt dizzy breathless, and sick.
    c. She felt dizzy, breathless, sick.
    d. She felt dizzy, breathless, and sick.

2. What change, if any, should be made to sentence 14?

    a. No change
    b. Add a comma after times
    c. Add a comma after minute
    d. Remove the parentheses around cramming

3. What change, if any, should be made to sentence 17?

    a. No change
    b. Change the word embedding to embed
    c. Add a comma after information
    d. Remove the comma after brain

4. What change, if any, should be made to sentence 20?

    a. No change
    b. Remove the comma after fun
    c. Add a comma after also
    d. Remove the word It

5. What change, if any, should be made to sentence 27?

    a. No change
    b. Change the word there to their
    c. Remove the comma after appear
    d. Add a comma after themselves

6. Which of the following is the correct punctuation of sentence 39?

   a. This can be done out loud or silently either way, it creates a positive attitude and outlook, that can reduce anxiety.

   b. This can be done out loud or silently; either way it creates a positive attitude and outlook that can reduce anxiety.

   c. This can be done out loud or silently; either way, it creates a positive attitude and outlook, that can reduce anxiety.

   d. This can be done out loud or silently; either way, it creates a positive attitude and outlook that can reduce anxiety.

7. What change, if any, should be made to sentence 44?

   a. No change

   b. Remove the commas around practice makes perfect

   c. Remove the word practice before triumph

   d. Add a comma after success

8. What change, if any, should be made to sentence 45?

   a. No change

   b. Remove the comma after problem

   c. Change the word an to a

   d. Change the word imaginated to imagined

9. What change, if any, should be made to sentence 49?

   a. No-change

   b. Change selftalk to self-talk

   c. Change atmosphere to atmusphere

   d. Add a comma after create

Questions 10 – 18 pertain to the following story:

The Memory Quilt

(1) Kevin had been saving his allowance for months to buy a new bike. (2) Now he was within a few dollars of his goal, and Grandma Ruth had offered to pay him to clean out her attic. (3) Kevin was excited. (4) The new bike was practically his!

(5) Early Saturday morning, Kevin's mom dropped him off at Grandma Ruth's house. (6) Grandma Ruth hugged him. (7) Then she walked upstairs with him and pointed him to a narrow latter that led up to the attic.

(8) "It's a mess up there," she warned. (9) "If you have any questions about anything, just ask. (10) Most of it is old junk, though. (11) You can sort things I won't want to keep into two piles—one to throw away and the other to donate to charity."

(12) Kevin climbed the ladder and looked around. (13) Boxes and piles of old pictures and records and clothes littered the floor. (14) It was a big job. (15) He picked up a painting of flowers in a chipped wooden frame. (16) It didnt look important, but Kevin thought he should check.

(17) "Grandma Ruth," he called, climbing down the ladder with the picture. "Is this important?"

- 162 -

(18) Grandma Ruth came out of her room and chuckled. (19) "No, Kevin. (20) Your grandfather and I bought that old picture at a yard sale years ago. (21) Put it in the pile to donate to charity."

(22) Kevin climbed back up the ladder. (23) He put the picture on the floor to start a pile for charity. (24) Then he picked up an old, rusty toolbox. (25) Like the old picture, it didn't look important, but Kevin thought he should check, just to make sure.

(26) "Grandma Ruth," he called again, climbing down the ladder with the toolbox. (27) "Is this important?"

(28) Grandma Ruth laughed gently. (29) "No, Kevin, your grandfather bought that toolbox when we bought this old house. (30) He was quite the handyman. (31) But I have no use for it now. (32) Put it in the pile to donate. (33) And Kevin?"

(34) "Yes, Grandma Ruth?"

(35) "You don't have to check with me about each thing. (36) If it looks old and unused, you can donate it or throw it away. (37) I trust your judgment. (38) But you can still ask if you have any questions." (39) She winked at Kevin and went back into her room.

(40) Kevin climbed back up the ladder. (41) He sorted through the piles quickly. (42) He climbed down and ate tuna fish sandwiches with Grandma Ruth in the dining room. (43) After lunch, she gave him some boxes to take up to the attic. (44) She told him to box up and carry down the items to be donated to charity. (45)

(46) Kevin made his way akwardly back to the attic, carrying the boxes. (47) He packed things up and sorted through piles until just before 4 pm, when his mom was coming to pick him up. (48) The last item he grabbed was a faded, dusty quilt. (49) He turned it over and studied it carefully. (50) It was worn, and it seemed like it hadn't been used in a long time. (51) Kevin threw it into a charity box and closed the top. (52) Then he began carrying boxes down the ladder.

(53) Kevin's mom drove him by the Goodwill store on the way home. (54) Together they unloaded the boxes of items to be donated. (55) Then they headed home, where Kevin fell asleep right after dinner. (56) He was exhausted from his hard work.

(57) On Sunday afternoon, Kevin went back to Grandma Ruth's house to finish cleanup out the attic. (58) The piles were sparser now, but they still popped up from the dusty floor like wayward molehills. (59) He got right to work, sorting, boxing things up, and neatly stacking the items to be kept.

(60) Halfway through the afternoon, Grandma Ruth called Kevin down for cookies and milk.

(61) "Kevin have you seen my old patchwork quilt up in the attic?" Grandma Ruth asked. (62) "I can't seem to find it anywhere. (63) I made that quilt from your grandfather's old work shirts and your mom's first baby blanket and the tablecloth I got at my wedding. (64) There are so many memories in that quilt."

(65) Kevin gulped. (66) He didn't want to lie to Grandma Ruth, but he couldn't tell her he donated her precious quilt to charity. (67) She would kill him!

- 163 -

(68) "I'll look for it when I go back up," he promised, knowing it wasn't there.

(69) At the end of the afternoon, Kevin was done cleaning the attic. (70) He carried the last box down the ladder.

(71) "Did you see my quilt up there?" Grandma Ruth asked.

(72) "No," Kevin said, half-truthfully.

(73) "I wonder where it could be," Grandma Ruth said.

(74) When Kevin and his mom stopped at the Goodwill store to donate the last set of boxes, Kevin asked if he ran inside. (75) He dashed in and browsed the shelves carefully. (76) Then he saw it. (77) It was stuffed between two stacks of throw pillows. (78) It was almost hidden, but unmistakable. (79) He pulled out the quilt and checked the price.

(80) Kevin's heart fell. (81) Paying for the quilt would mean he would have to wait another month or two to buy his bike. (82) If he just went home, no one would ever know about his mistake. (83) But he knew that would be wrong. (84) Buying the quilt back was the right thing to do. (85) Kevin paid for the quilt and hurried back to the car.

(86) Kevin's mom looked at the quilt with surprise. (87) "Isn't that Grandma Ruth's memory quilt?"

(88) Kevin nodded glumly. (89) He told his mom the whole story. (90) Then he said he needed to go back to Grandma Ruth's house to tell her the truth.

(91) "I'm proud of you" Kevin's mom said, as she turned the car around. (92) "Let's go give Grandma Ruth back her memories."

10. What change, if any, should be made to sentence 7?
    a. No change
    b. Change the word led to leads
    c. Change the word latter to ladder
    d. Change the word pointed to points

11. What change, if any, should be made to sentence 16?
    a. No change
    b. Add an apostrophe in the word didnt
    c. Remove the comma after important
    d. Add a comma after thought

12. What change, if any, should be made to sentence 29?
    a. No change
    b. Add parentheses after house.
    c. Change your to you're
    d. Add a comma after toolbox

13. Where is the best place for the following sentence?
By lunchtime, he was almost halfway done.

a. Between sentence 12 and 13
b. Between sentence 22 and 23
c. Between sentence 61 and 62
d. Between sentence 41 and 42

14. What change, if any, should be made to sentence 46?

a. No change
b. Add a comma after way
c. Change akwardly to awkwardly
d. Change carrying to carying

15. What change, if any, can be made to sentence 57?

a. No change
b. Change Ruth's to Ruths
c. Change Sunday to sunday
d. Change cleanup to cleaning

16. Which of the following sentences shows the correct punctuation of sentence 61?

a. "Kevin have you seen my old patchwork quilt up in the attic?" Grandma Ruth asked.
b. "Kevin, have you seen my old patchwork quilt up in the attic?" Grandma Ruth asked.
c. "Kevin have you seen my old patchwork quilt up in the attic," Grandma Ruth asked?
d. "Kevin, have you seen my old patchwork quilt up in the attic." Grandma Ruth asked?

17. What change, if any, can be made to sentence 74?

a. No change
b. Change the word ran to could run
c. Remove the comma after boxes
d. Add a comma after store

18. What change, if any, can be made to sentence 91?

a. No change
b. Remove the comma after said
c. Remove the apostrophe in I'm
d. Add a comma between you and "

Questions 19 – 27 pertain to the following article:

Like Riding a Kite

(1) Imagine soaring high above the earth. (2) There is no engine, no fuselage beneath you. (3) There is only you, your glider, the wind, and the sky. (4) It's like riding a kite with no strings attached rising and falling on the breeze like a bird. (5) It is freedom and thrill and ultimate pleasure. (6) This is the world of hang gliding.

(7) While many people have a general idea of what hang gliding is all about, few really understand the sport. (8) Most people don't realize a majestic glider can be collapsed to the size of a duffel bag. (9) Few people know that gliders can stay afloat for hours and that the world record distance for a single glider flight is nearly 190 miles. (10) Even fewer people realize that a hang glider can actually climb in the sky, even without an engine. (11)

- 165 -

In California in the 1980s, one expert glider pilot gained more than 14000 feet of altitude after takeoff! (12) Hang gliders have mind-boggling capabilities.

(13) The amazing sport of hang gliding has a rich history dating back to the 1890s. (14) In 1891, the first hang glider was invented by Otto Lilienthal in Germany. (15) It was made of wood and cloth, weighed 40 pounds, was 23 feet wide, and could go about 35 miles per hour (mph) at an altitude of 100 feet. (16) British inventor Percy Picher also built gliders with similar features in the late 1890s. (17) Unfortunately, both inventors were killed in glider crashes before their designs were perfected. (18) With the element of danger involved in early hang gliding—and with the advent of airplane flight by the Wright brothers in 1903—many people lost interest in hang gliding.

(19) After the end of World War II, however, many military-trained pilots wanted to keep flying. (20) Airplanes were too expensive for most people, so the sport of hang gliding was reborn. (21) Through invention and innovation, new designs for hang gliders began to emerge. (22) These included new materials and designs for glider construction and the addition of a control bar to improve safety. (23) The basic design for today's hang gliders premiered at a meet in California in 1971. (24) It included a broad, flexible wing on a sturdy frame with a control bar and a seat or safety harness.

(25) Since 1971 few major design changes have been made to hang gliders, although as new materials for construction become available, minor changes are made to improve flight. (26) Modern sails range from 13 to 28 feet across. (27) They are made of durable, lightweight, manmade fabric—such as nylon—and are designed to flex in shape and tension based on the wind. (28)The sail is attached to a frame made from aluminum tubing. (29) The frame includes a control bar, shaped like a rounded triangle and used for steering. (30) Suspended from the frame is a harness or seat to improve pilot comfort and safety.

(31) Another way pilots improve comfort and safety is through the use of proper gear and equipment. (32) Pilots should wear light, protective clothing and gloves designed for hang gliding. (33) A helmet is also an important safety component. (34) In addition, pilots need special instruments that are used during flight. (35) These tools help measure thermals, the warm air currents used to lift and propel gliders through the air.

(36) Thermals are important to both taking off and staying aloft, but they aren't the only factor in flight.(37) Modern gliders weigh about 35 pounds and are special balanced to a pilot's weight and preferences. (38) To take off, the pilot is secured in the glider and then runs off the edge of a large hill or cliff, where thermals catch the glider and lift it into the air. (39) If the wind is sustained at 12 mph or above, the pilot may even be able to take off without running. (40) Once the glider is airborne, the pilot steers by shifting his/her weight and using the control bar. (41) Each glider has its own unique feel, and a pilot must know the glider well to achieve a safe takeoff, flight, and landing.

(42) They must yield the right of way to any aircraft in distress and all hot air balloons. (43) Pilots of hang gliders do not need to be licensed, but they must obey all rules and laws for flying. (44) In addition to knowing the unique feel of the glider, a pilot must know the safety rules of the sky to have a safe flight. (45) Hang glider pilots should never fly in bad weather or high winds. (46) They must never intentionally fly into a cloud or a flock of birds. (47) Finally, hang glider pilots should stay at least five miles away from airports

during flight and at least 100 foot from buildings, telephone wires and poles, populated places, and crowds.

(48) Throughout history, mankind has looked for a way to sore with the birds across the canvas of the sky. (49) Hang gliding offers that opportunity. (50) With modern features and equipment, and with proper training in techniques and the rules of the sky, hang glider pilots can safely experience the thrill of flight. (51) In a glider, the pilot is one with the breeze, the sunlight, the world itself. (52) Hang gliding is truly like riding a kite through the expense of the heavens.

19. What change, if any, should be made to sentence 4?
   a. No change
   b. Add a comma after attached
   c. Add a comma after kite
   d. Add a comma after breeze

20. What change, if any, should be made to sentence 9?
   a. No change
   b. Add a comma after flight
   c. Change the word afloat to aloft
   d. Change the word Few to Many

21. Which of the following is the best way to punctuate sentence 11?
   a. In California in the 1980s one expert glider pilot gained more than 14000 feet of altitude after takeoff!
   b. In California in the 1980s one expert glider pilot gained more than 14,000 feet of altitude after takeoff.
   c. In California, in the 1980s one expert glider pilot gained more than 14000 feet of altitude after takeoff.
   d. In California, in the 1980s, one expert glider pilot gained more than 14,000 feet of altitude after takeoff!

22. What change, if any, should be made to sentence 25?
   a. No change
   b. Remove the comma after gliders
   c. Add a comma after 1971
   d. Change the word although to though

23. Which of the following would be the best way to combine sentences 33 and 34?
   a. A helmet is also an important safety component, in addition, pilots need special instruments that are used during flight.
   b. A helmet is also an important safety component, as well as special instruments that pilots use during flight.
   c. A helmet is also an important safety component, pilots also need special instruments that are used during flight.
   d. A helmet is also an important safety component, and pilots use special instruments during flight.

24. Which sentence belongs at the beginning of paragraph 6?
    a. Sentence 42
    b. Sentence 43
    c. Sentence 44
    d. Sentence 45

25. What change, if any, should be made to sentence 47?
    a. No change
    b. Change the word foot to feet
    c. Remove the comma after finally
    d. Change the word should to could

26. What change, if any, should be made to sentence 48?
    a. No change
    b. Change the word mankind to man-kind
    c. Change the word across to around
    d. Change the word sore to soar

27. What change, if any, should be made to sentence 52?
    a. No change
    b. Change the word expense to expanse
    c. Add a comma after like
    d. Change the word truly to truely

Questions 28– 35pertain to the following passage:

Summer's Heat

(1) I remember the day as if it were yesterday. (2) It was Saturday afternoon and cloudless. (3) The sun beat down upon my face, even through the chain link fenced dugout. (4) It was so hot that I could feel my skin burning, and I was sweating, even though I wasn't on the field. (5) I sat on the bench with a jug of water at my feet and a fistful of sunflower seeds. (6) We were losing, three to one. (7) I looked at our right fielder Johnny who was fanning his face with his glove as he was getting ready for the play.

(8) The ball was hit to the third basemen, and he got the last out of the inning at first base. (9) The team ran into a huddle, and our coach told us to keep our eye on the ball. (10) "Concentrate," he said.

(11) Philip hit the ball to the fence and was stopped on second base by the coaches. (12) We were all shouting and very happy with his double. (13) The next batter bunted the ball to the pitcher, and moved Philip to third base. (14) Johnny then came to the plate and hit a double. (15) Philip scored, and we were one run away, from tying the game.

(16) "Max!" the coach shouted.

(17) I turned my head and was shocked to see that I wasn't imagining things. (18) Coach was pointing right at me.

(19) "You're up," he said.

(20) I threw my sunflower seeds to the ground, stuffed my helmet onto my head, and grabbed my favorite bat. (21) I took two practice swings and was ready for the pitcher.

(22) I hit two foul balls over the side fences. (23) They were hard, and flew for a long time before ever hitting the ground. (24) I also needed to work on my fielding, especially catching fly balls. (25) I was going to get Johnny to home plate. (26) I just needed one good pitch.

(27) The pitcher looked down at his feet and then stared into my eyes. (28) I stared back. (29) It was like there was no one else on the field. (30) It was just us. (31) He started his windup, and I dug my feet into the ground and adjusted my grip on the bat. (32) The ball came in and I swung at it as hard as I could.

(33) I was confused. (34) I didn't feel anything.

(35) "Strike three!" the umpire yelled behind me.

(36) I was out.

(37) Bradley came up after me and we ended up losing the game three to two.

(38) The coaches told us we played a good game. (39) They said that it was a team effort and that we should be proud of ourselves. (40) My mom told me it was not my fault. (41) "It was no one's fault," she said. (42) It is just a game.

(43) But it was not just a game to me. (44) I felt like I had let everyone down and disappointed all of my teammates. (45) It was the last game of the season, and we lost.

(46) I decided at that moment to spend my summer vacation training. (47) I was going to do nothing but practice baseball. (48) I spent two weeks outside, with just my baseball bat and a bucket of balls. (49) I hit until it was dark and my mom force me to come inside and eat dinner. (50) When I asked her if we could install some lights into the backyard so that I could see and practice more, she looked at me with a very stern face and said the most horrible sentence.

(51) "No more baseball for the rest of the summer."

(52) My heart dropped. (53) I felt sick to my stomach and filled with anger.

(54) "How can you do this to me?" I shouted back.

(55) "There is more to life than baseball," she said. (56) "I want you to enjoy spending the summer playing with your friends."

(57) She then grounded me for the weekend for shouting at her.

(58) After a few days without baseball, I realized how fun it was to be a regular kid and spent time with my friends, swimming in the pool, fishing in the lake, and climbing trees. (59) Once, someone suggested we play some baseball, and we gathered some of our friends together and played a game in the park. (60) We didn't keep score, and had fun just playing. (61) It was a great summer.

(62) When baseball season came around again, I played center field. (63) My first time up to bat, I smiled. (64) I was having fun. (65) The pitch came and I swung hard. (66) The ball landed on the other side of the fence, and I ran around the bases to cheers after hitting my first homerun.

28. What change, if any, should be made to sentence 7?

  a. No change
  b. Add commas before and after Johnny
  c. Change the word fanning to faning
  d. Change the words who was to which was

29. What change, if any, should be made to sentence 9?

  a. No change
  b. Add comma after us
  c. Change the word huddle to hurdle
  d. Remove the comma after huddle

30. What change, if any, should be made to sentence 15?

  a. No change
  b. Change the words we were to we're
  c. Remove the comma after scored
  d. Remove the comma after away

31. Which of the following sentences does not belong or is out of place in the story?

  a. Sentence 15
  b. Sentence 51
  c. Sentence 24
  d. Sentence 21

32. What change, if any, should be made to sentence 37?

  a. No change
  b. Change the word two to one
  c. Change the word came to comes up
  d. Add a comma after game

33. Which of the following shows the correct punctuation of sentences 41 and 42?

  a. "It was no one's fault," she said. It is just a game.
  b. "It was no one's fault," she said. "It is just a game."
  c. "It was no ones fault," she said. "It is just a game."
  d. "It was no one's fault" she said. "It is just a game."

34. What change, if any, should be made to sentence 49?

  a. No change
  b. Change the word force to forced
  c. Change the word hit to was hitting
  d. Change the word was to is

- 170 -

35. What change, if any, should be made to sentence 58?

    a. No change

    b. Remove the comma after baseball

    c. Change the word spent to spend

    d. Change the word realized to began realizing

Answers and Explanations

1. D: The sentence contains a list which should be separated by commas and include an *and* before the last thing in the list.

2. B. A comma is needed here to separate an independent and a dependent clause.

3. B: The word *embedding* is the present participle of the word embed. The present participle is only needed in certain situations. It is most commonly used as part of the continuous form of a verb, or after verbs of movement/position. This does not fall into any of the circumstances where a present participle should be used.

4. A: This sentence is grammatically correct.

5. B: The word should be *their* because *their* shows possession. In this case it is *their* eyes.

6. D: In this case a semicolon is used to link two independent clauses with closely related ideas. Then treat the second part like it is its own sentence. The words *either way* are an introduction that need to be set apart from the rest of the sentence with a comma. There is no comma needed after *outlook*.

7. C: The word *practice* is not needed in this sentence. The sentence makes more sense and reads more fluently without it.

8. D: *Imaginated* is not a word. The word should be *imagined*.

9. B: The word *selftalk* is not a word. Instead it is two words put together to make a compound word that requires a hyphen to separate each of the words.

10. C: The definition of the word *latter* is, situated or occurring nearer to the end of something than to the beginning. In this story Kevin was climbing up a *ladder*, which is a structure consisting of a series of bars or steps between two upright lengths of wood, metal, or rope, used for climbing up or down something.

11. B: The word *didn't* is a contraction, which is a shortened version of the written and spoken forms of a word, syllable, or word group, created by omission of internal letters. These letters are replaced with an apostrophe.

12. A: No change is needed. This sentence is grammatically correct.

13. D: This spot makes the most sense because sentence 42 begins talking about what he ate for lunch.

14. C: The correct way to spell the word is *awkwardly*.

15. D: The word *cleanup* is a noun. Instead there needs to be a verb here. The correct verb is the present participle of the word *clean*, which is *cleaning*.

16. B: The question mark needs to be inside the parentheses where the question is being asked. There needs to be a comma after Kevin to set the introductory phrase apart from the rest of the sentence.

17. B: *Ran* is the past tense of the verb *run*. In this case Kevin is asking if he can run inside. It is not past tense.

18. D: There needs to be a comma here to separate the quote from the rest of the sentence. Also remember that quotes go outside of the punctuation.

19. B: A comma should be used here to separate two independent clauses.

20. C: The correct word here is *aloft*. *Afloat* means to be floating on water. While, *aloft* means to be up in the air. Hang gliders fly through the air.

21. D: The exclamation point is appropriate here because they are speaking with strong feeling about such amazing feat. Commas are used in numbers larger than three digits to make them easier to read. The commas at the beginning of the sentence set apart introductory phrases.

22. C: There needs to be a comma after *1971* to separate the introductory phrase from the rest of the sentence.

23. B: This sentence has the correct punctuation as well as the correct transition words to join the two sentences.

24. C: This sentence belongs at the beginning of the paragraph because it is a transition sentence. It mentions the *unique feel* that was discussed in the last paragraph and links it to the new topic of *safety rules*.

25. B: *Feet* is the plural form of *foot*. In this case *feet* is correct because we are talking about *100 feet*.

26. D: The word *sore* refers to a painful or aching part of one's body. The correct word to use here is *soar*. Which means to fly or rise high in the air.

27. B: An *expense* is the cost required for something. The correct word here is *expanse*, which means the area of something. It is referring to the great area of the heavens.

28. B: In this case commas are used to set off nonessential words. The sentence still makes sense if you

29. A: No change is needed. This sentence is grammatically correct.

30. D: There is no need for the sentence to be separated right here, therefore there should be no comma

31. C: This sentence could belong in the story but it does not belong where it is. He is in the middle of an at bat, trying to get the runner home, and this sentence is about fielding.

32. D: There needs to be a comma here to separate the independent and dependent clause.

33. B: The word *one's* needs the apostrophe to show possession. Also it should include two different sets of parentheses. The words *she said* do not go in the parentheses.

34. B: The sentence is written in past tense. The word should be *forced*, which is the past tense of *force*.

35. C: This sentence is written in the present tense so the word should be *spend* instead of the past tense *spent*.

Writing

Producing clear and coherent writing

The first step to producing clear and coherent writing is to plan what you want to write about, what your purpose will be, and who your audience will be. Do you want to explain an idea? Do you want to persuade your audience? Do you want to entertain? These are all considerations when deciding on a purpose. Once you have settled on a purpose, you will need to develop the presentation by figuring out how to organize it and deciding on a style. A style should be chosen that fits with the purpose of the text and its audience. If you are writing a formal report, you need to adopt a formal style of writing. However, if you are writing something more casual, and your audience expects a casual approach, then there is no need for a formal style. Whatever the purpose or audience, your text should include proper English grammar and have a beginning, middle, and ending.

Constructive criticism

Writing is an ongoing process in that it needs to be revised, edited and possibly rewritten before it is completed. This process can be a difficult one, so it is wise to have the support of peers and adults who can objectively critique your work. The first thing to do when writing a text is to know what you want to say and then write a rough draft. Sit with it for a few hours or days, and then revisit it and make any changes that you think will improve it. Then ask a friend or an adult, a teacher perhaps, to read the text and critique it. Their feedback will be very useful, and you will probably want to revise or rewrite based on what they say. At some point, the text may need to be edited for improper language. Make sure that your use of pronouns is precise and correct and that you double check your spelling before you are finished.

Using the internet

The technology of the Internet has changed the way in which writing can be produced and published. Self-publishing sites abound on the Internet and many people produce e-books with ease. But that is just one aspect. For students, technology allows for easy access to sources used in a writing project. These sources can be cited by listing the URL, title, author, and date retrieved. Once written, you can post your writing on a blog and then you can discuss it in one of the many chat rooms and topic websites. These tools allow for an unprecedented exchange of information. In addition, many free tools are accessible that provide software to allow people to work together on a wide variety of projects, no matter how far apart they are geographically. Students can find discussion groups, file sharing networks, social networking sites, blogs and task management sites, all of which foster interaction and collaboration.

Conducting a short research project

To conduct a short research project to answer a question, it is best to begin by creating a list of key words that can be entered into an Internet search engine to find the information you are seeking from an online source, such as an encyclopedia, journals, magazines, and other available sources. You may have to refine and refocus your inquiry if you do not find the exact information you want—sometimes a simple rewriting of the keyword will bring up more information than what appeared in the first search. Whatever information you plan to use to answer the question should be cited correctly following the standards of the MLA (Modern Language Association).

Your teacher wants you to find the answer to the question, "Who discovered America?" Discuss how to go about finding the answer.

The best way to learn who discovered America is to start with an Internet search. You would need to come up with keywords for a search engine. You could simply type in the question for a start and that would lead to an enormous amount of information. You could change the keywords by searching for "America discoverer," or "American discovery" to see if this yields other information. Check out the websites and make sure they are reliable and accredited. Pick sites that are related to historic groups or affiliated with colleges or universities or other credible sources. And be sure to credit your sources when you write your answer.

Gathering relevant information from multiple print and digital sources

After doing research through an online search for information on a topic and a visit to the school library for research on the same subject in the print resources there, you will need to make a list of your sources with the information you gathered from each and review the sources to see whether they are credible. Credible sources will have legitimacy to them; they could be related to a university, a historic society, or a scientific group. Delete any sources that are suspect. Then, when you start to write your essay, make sure you do not copy any of the information from a site or print source verbatim; that is, you need to paraphrase the information so that it is not plagiarized. By putting your own spin on the material, avoiding such plagiarism can usually be accomplished fairly easily. You may wish to include quotations from experts, in which case you must cite the quote. At the end of your paper, you should include all sources and properly cite them using the MLA (Modern Language Association) standards.

Importance of varying sentence patterns when writing

Readers become bored with what they are reading if the way in which it is written is dull and repetitive. One short sentence after another will not appeal to the average reader, nor would one long sentence after another. Written text should have variety. Sentences should be both simple and complex and the syntax should change as you write. This gives the writing life and rhythm. You can interject variety by combining multiple short sentences into one long sentence through the use of clauses and phrases. Mix in a handful of direct short sentences to break up a pattern of too many long sentences. A good tip is to read what you have written aloud and see if it has a pleasing rhythm.

Discuss how to rewrite the sentences below to make them more varied:

> Andre and Susan went to Cape Cod last week. They hoped to see a cranberry harvest. But they arrived too early in the season. The harvest would not take place for another month. They were disappointed when they left.

All of the sentences in the excerpt are about the same length and follow the same pattern. They are monotonous because of a lack of variety. The use of clauses and phrases to combine information would improve the flow of the words. One way that they could be rewritten to make them more interesting is the following:

> Andre and Susan went to Cape Cod last week hoping to see a cranberry harvest. They were disappointed, however, because the harvest would not take place for another month. They arrived too early in the season.

This version has rhythm and variety in the sentences. A reader would be more interested in reading the entire excerpt because of this.

Importance of maintaining a consistent style and tone

When writing, it is important to maintain a consistent style and tone. For instance, if you are writing a formal report, you should maintain a formal style and tone of writing. To suddenly have a section of the paper that uses informal language and a casual tone would not fit into the completed text. In the same manner, if you are writing a story about a ten-year-old girl, the language that you have her use should be consistent with words that she would understand. The style and tone of a story tell you a lot about the narrator, so it is important to be consistent in order for the reader to understand what you are attempting to say.

Ways the approach used in a poem on a subject might be different from the approach used to write a story about the same subject

Poetry is very different from stories; poems do not usually tell a story or have many characters, although some do. Poems are more concerned about creating a mood, drawing a picture, and giving a reader images that will have an emotional effect. Stories can also set moods and have an emotional effect, but the intent of a story is to describe something that happened. Most stories have plots and characters who reveal themselves and interact with the events in the story. Both poems and stories can have themes. For instance, a poem about a walk in the woods might not have much action, but it would probably create a sensation of what it feels like to be walking in the woods. A story about walking in the woods would most likely address not only the setting, but also the events that occur during the walk and how the characters react to them.

Using critical reading skills

When reading nonfiction pieces, you should analyze the author's point of view. Then you need to assess the author's claims and see if the evidence given is sound and relevant. In a way, you will need to be a detective. This requires using critical reading skills. You need to figure out if the reasoning is sound. Ask yourself if what the author says is based on fact or unjustified opinion. Distinguish between statements by determining if they are based on fact or opinion. Check the sources that are cited. Look for evidence of bias, omissions and stereotypes; their presence severely distorts a work of nonfiction.

Making writing a habit

Writing is important both in school and in life. It is essential to learn to write routinely so that writing comes easily and smoothly. You can make writing a habit by doing it every day in some way. Certainly it is true that the more you write the better your writing will become. Familiarize yourself with the process of writing—taking notes, writing drafts, rewriting, editing, and revising once again—and you will come to understand the concept of writing for different kinds of audiences. Some writing needs to be longer and more thoroughly researched. Other writing can be shorter. It depends on the topic, the audience, and how complex you wish to be. Learning the skills necessary to master the art of writing for specific reasons will lead to greater recognition in any field you choose.

Persuasive Text

Introducing claims and organizing reasons and evidence that support the claims clearly

When introducing claims in a persuasive text, be sure that the claim is thoroughly researched and thought through. You should have clear evidence that your claim is valid. The best way to do this is to make notes or an outline. When writing, organize your passage so that your claim comes first and then list the reasons and evidence that you have to support the claim. Make sure the reasons and evidence follow from each other so that they are in a clear order. Delete any claims that you cannot verify by reliable outside sources. By doing this you will be able to write a convincing presentation based on sound research.

Analyze the claim made in the statement below:

> The idea of building a minor league baseball stadium is a good one. It could be used not only by a farm team, but also for concerts. It is sure to attract people and help the town's economy. So vote yes at the polls on the referendum.

This claim may or may not be valid. While the statement says that the baseball stadium will attract people and be good for the town's economy, it does not provide any concrete evidence for the claim. There is no way to know whether building a baseball stadium would attract people. There are no facts or figures from other places that have already built a similar stadium, so the evidence is not based on anything credible. When making a claim, the argument should be well researched and sources used to back up the claim and make it a valid one. This is not the case in the statement that was given.

When making a claim you will need to research arguments in support of it that come from trustworthy sources. It is not enough to research a claim on the Internet because many Internet sources are dubious. If you are doing research on the Internet, then you will need to find information that can be verified by several objective sites. Another avenue is to find authorities in a field that have written or spoken on the topic that you are presenting so that you can quote these people. These authorities should have substantial degrees in their field as well as a vast experience so that their opinions will have credence and respect. Be sure to cite any information that you use to support a claim correctly. And make sure to present your arguments in a logical manner so that they will be easily understood by the listener or reader.

Use words, phrases and clauses to clarify the relationship between claims and reasons

When writing, it is important to phrase your sentences so that the relationship between claims and reasons is clear. Words or phrases such as "because," "since, "as a result of," and "as a consequence" or "consequently" all suggest a causality that may exist between a claim and a reason. Clauses can also be utilized to show relationships. For example, the sentence "We are going to lose the election as a result of not working hard enough to convince the public" shows causality between the claim and the reason. When writing, make sure to recheck your sentences to ensure that there is a natural flow and that the relationships between claims and reasons are clear and logical.

Choose which of the following words fits best in the blank and why: "otherwise" or "because:"

> The jury found the defendant not guilty _____ the testimony of the eyewitness was weak.

"Because" is the correct choice because it shows a cause and effect relationship. "Otherwise" shows a relationship of contrast which is not the case here. It is important to understand the relationship between what happened as a result of something else. Using the correct linking word clarifies meaning and gives your sentences a logical flow. "Otherwise" suggests a relationship that exists between opposing possibilities. But this is not the case here. Using the word "because" gives the sentence a natural and logical flow.

Formal style

When writing any kind of formal paper, a *formal style* of writing needs to be established and maintained throughout. A formal writing style includes the use of the third person, rather than first or second person. This lends a more serious and objective tone to a paper; personal feelings have little place in formal writing. A formal style also requires proper English conventions as well as language that is professional and specific. Generally idioms and contractions have no place when using a formal writing style, which requires that the author be objective and professional.

Read the following lines. Suggest how to make them more formal:

> Turtles are something I like. They're reptiles and breathe. They have lungs like me. Some turtles breathe underwater. I've read that turtles eat many things like insects and fish and fruit too! Some turtles sleep underwater too.

The style of the passage is very informal and personalized; the first person is used exclusively. Sentences are all short and simple, and there is little substance.

Here is one way to rewrite it:

> Turtles are interesting animals. They are reptiles and they breathe. They have lungs like humans do. Some turtles breathe underwater. They may sleep underwater too. They eat many things, including insects, fish, and fruit.

To give the passage a more formal tone, the first person is replaced by the third person. The organization is better because related information is put together, such as the fact that some turtles can both breathe and sleep underwater. The contraction was eliminated, as well as the reference to having lungs "like me." The exclamation mark also does not have a place in formal writing because it suggests feelings rather than logic.

Good concluding statement

It is important that a writer include a good concluding statement or section that follows from an argument in order to sum up a claim and review the intention of the text. This will give the audience a sense of closure. The conclusion or section should go over the most important points that were made in the persuasive text as well as the reasons and arguments made by the author in a brief form. The conclusion should make the reader feel that he or she has a firm understanding of the issue. A good conclusion is important to the effectiveness of a text.

Veronica is writing a persuasive passage on why she believes that students should go to school all year long. She needs a concluding statement. Describe how she should go about writing a conclusion.

Veronica should review the arguments that she has made about what the benefits of going to school all year long are and the sources that she used to prove her point. She should also make a general statement about why she feels it would be a good idea. A personal appeal and an explanation of the benefits this approach would have could be used. It is probably best not to include too much about opposing points of view in the conclusion. The conclusion that Veronica writes should give the reader a sense of closure and satisfaction. It should not introduce new material or leave items open for further discussion.

Informational or Explanatory Text

Introducing a topic

When writing an informational or explanatory text, the author will need to introduce the topic that the text will be about. There are numerous strategies that can help improve the reader's comprehension of the subject. An author may choose to define key words that a reader may not be familiar with, classify information or compare and contrast it, or use a cause and effect relationship in the report. Charts and tables are extremely useful for displaying complicated information and the use of headings can help signify where certain information will be found. Multimedia devices, including video and audio, can also improve the way in which an author displays his material because they are appealing to the audience or reader.

Sara is writing a report on sea turtles. She has researched the various dangers that they face: their predators, the difficulties they encounter in their life cycle starting with their birth, their migration to the ocean, and the dangers that await them as they mature. She is unsure of how to organize her report.
Explain which organization pattern would be the best choice for her and why.

A cause and effect order would seem to be the best idea for Sara because she would be able to identify the causes and effects of the dangers that sea turtles encounter. She could organize the report so that each paragraph deals with a different threat, using headings to identify what would be in each section. A chart would also be useful because it puts the same information in a clear format so that readers would be able to refer to it. She might also consider using a video showing baby turtles migrating towards the open sea, which would give her audience an even greater understanding of the turtles' plight.

Developing a topic

To develop a topic in an informational or explanatory text, an author needs to use relevant facts that support details related to the main topic. The topic may be included in a topic sentence or opening statement and then followed by supporting details. Some of the supporting details should be concrete facts that have been researched and confirmed. Quotations of experts in the field of the topic are another good source for supporting material. Quoting experts gives variety and credence to a text. Examples, charts, and multimedia techniques can also be used to enhance the presentation, but these extras should not be used as a substitute for solid supporting details.

Analyze the beginning of this informational text and tell what could be added to improve it:

The journey of the salmon from salt water to fresh water to breed is one of the wonders of nature. This journey, called the salmon run, is difficult because the fish must swim upriver against the current. Some even leap up waterfalls as they make their way back to their original breeding grounds.

This seems like a good start to an informational text. The first sentence establishes the topic. It tells what the report is going to be about. It also includes two supporting details to tell more about the topic. This is one way to introduce and develop a topic in a report or other informational or explanatory text. What should come next are more supporting details and also sources for the information that is cited; a quotation from an authority of the salmon run would make the report stronger and give it credence. Some statistics, facts, figures about how many salmon make the run each year and how many survive would also be of interest.

Using appropriate transitions

When writing an informational or explanatory text it is important to use appropriate transitions that will clarify the relationships among ideas and concepts. For example, to show causality between ideas, use transition words or phrases, such as "therefore," "consequently," and "as a result of." To show comparison or contrast relationships, words such as "however," "on the other hand," "but," "in contrast," and "similarly" should be used. Transition words and expressions to introduce examples include "for example," "for instance," "namely" and "that is." The order of importance can also be shown through transitions, such as "at first," "former," "latter," "primarily" and "second."

Importance of using precise language and domain-specific vocabulary

When writing informational or explanatory texts it is of upmost importance to use precise language and domain-specific vocabulary to explain your main idea and supporting details. Generalized vocabulary will not help the audience grasp the points that you are attempting to make because they will not accurately reflect your main idea and supporting details. Domain-specific vocabulary is important to use because it will accurately describe or explain the ideas or processes that are central to your text. When you research a subject, make sure to familiarize yourself with any vocabulary that is involved in its explanation. Use context clues, dictionaries, or, if necessary, a technical dictionary to decode any words that you are not familiar with. Also include definitions of domain-specific vocabulary in your text to enlighten readers.

Establishing and maintaining a formal style

When writing an informational or explanatory text it is important to establish and maintain a formal style of writing. Do not use a colloquial or casual tone. It is necessary to use the third person and to make the sentences longer and more complex. It is also important not to use contractions when you write. A formal style announces that the writer is serious about his or her subject and wants to write an objective paper. This can be done by keeping the main ideas and supporting details clear, to the point, but as complex as they need to be. A formal style also means that the writer will not include a personal opinion that is not justified.

Discuss why the following excerpt is an example of formal writing:

> Richard Spruce found his life's work in the jungles of South America. Spruce grew up in a part of England that was filled with plants growing wild and free. His love of plants developed early. When he read a book about the Amazon jungle in Brazil, he decided to go there to study the area's plant life.

This is a good example of formal writing. It is objective and unbiased. The author uses the third person perspective, which formal writing is supposed to do. He sets out his main idea in the initial topic sentence, and then gives good supporting details. His sentences are somewhat complex and varied. He does not use any contractions, which are not used in formal writing, and the language is not colloquial or casual. The style of writing matches the subject. At the same time, the writing is not dull; the reader is intrigued and wants to learn more. Formal writing does not have to be uninteresting.

Importance of a concluding statement

A concluding statement or section that follows from and supports the information or explanation is important to a text because the conclusion helps to focus the important points in a text and also provides closure to the reader or audience. A good conclusion attempts to sum up the passage and any conclusions that the author makes so that the audience feels they have received a logical ending to the text. An effective conclusion gives the passage the weight it needs to have an effect. The conclusion should not make the reader feel that there is more information to follow, but rather set the tone for the ending of the topic.

Narratives

Establishing a context and introducing a narrator and/or characters

When writing a narrative, an author must establish the context of the story, which means he needs to set the stage for the story to begin. Sometimes this is done by establishing the setting of the story and then introducing a narrator and characters. Sometimes a character or the narrator is introduced first. A narrator and/or characters can be introduced in many ways: through the use of dialogue, through description, or through the reactions of the narrator or characters to an event. Whatever means an author chooses needs to call out to the audience so that they will be immediately interested in what is happening in the narrative. The beginning of a narrative must be compelling so that a reader will continue.

Discuss the introduction of the character in the following passage:

> Her parents named her Milagro, which means "miracle" in Spanish, but they called her Milly. She was a premature baby, very tiny, and it was a miracle that she survived. That was the beginning of her good fortune.

The author uses a dramatic way to introduce her character. She tells us that "Milagro" means "miracle" in Spanish. She tells us that it was a miracle that she survived her birth because she was born prematurely. She tells us that that was the beginning of her good fortune, a piece of information that tempts the reader to keep reading and find out more about Milagro's life. The way Milagro is introduced is dramatic because the author uses information to hint at what may come next. This is a form of foreshadowing. The author has established an interesting beginning with the way in which she introduces this character.

Sequence of events

A sequence of events in a narrative should come naturally and logically out of the action and the plot. The sequence should follow the natural flow of a dialogue or plot and enhance what happens in the story. This is generally the rule, although authors sometimes use a literary device called *flashback*, in which the sequence of events is presented out of order. A flashback shows the action that will take place in the future before the events that build up to it. But following a flashback, the order of events will return to normal. The order of events in a narrative is important in helping the reader understand the intent or message of a narrative. When reading a narrative, take note of the order in which events occur to give a broader understanding of the passage.

Techniques used by an author

Authors can choose from many techniques to bring their stories to life. Dialogue is an important tool; it not only tells you what is happening in a narrative, but it also suggests what a character's personality is like. The reader can tell from what a character says and how the character says it what the character feels about the events in a narrative or even what he feels about himself. Pacing is equally important; the pacing is the rhythm of a story. It can move slowly in one section and then speed up to build intensity. Descriptions that are vivid help the reader visualize what is happening and what a character is like. All of these techniques help color the experiences and events in a narrative and increase the receptivity of the reader.

Discuss the pacing in the following excerpt:

> The day was lazy and long and no one wanted to move around very much, even though they were supposedly hunting. And then, out of nowhere, a deer darted over the horizon. Joe and Neal jumped up. They were alert now. It was time to get going.

The pacing changes from a leisurely pace at the beginning to a quick pace. It parallels what is happening in the excerpt. At first there is nothing happening so the pace is slow and relaxed. But after the deer appears, the pace picks up and so does the action. The pace mirrors the plot. The pace is shown by the use of sentences. Long sentences give a slow feeling, while shorter sentences create a quicker pace and help build tension in the writing. A story's pacing creates its rhythm, and a reader should realize how that is affecting him.

Importance of transition words

Transition words are very important when writing a narrative. They can indicate a sequence of events and also signal shifts from one time frame or setting to another. Sequence words such as "first," "second," and "last" assist the reader in understanding the order in which events occur, which can be important to the flow of the plot. Words such as "then" or "next" also show the order in which events occur. "After a while" and "before this" are other sequence expressions. A change in setting can also be indicated. For instance, a passage may say, "At first we were sitting comfortably in the hotel lobby," but later on it might say, "after we talked, we went to the theater to watch the musical." This shows a shift in setting. When reading, notice transition words and their effect on the action.

Precise language

It is important to use precise language and descriptions that are lively and thought provoking so that a reader can gain insight into a character or situation. Details of the setting, what characters do, or the events in a narrative should be described in vivid and sensory language. The more moving the writing, the more moved the reader will be. Sensory language in particular helps convey the mood and feeling of the setting, situation, and characters. All of this will add to the development of a memorable theme. When reading, take care to notice the selection of words and phrases that an author employs in order to better comprehend the meaning of a narrative.

Read the excerpt and analyze the language:

> At dawn, in a stuffy and smoky second-class car in which five people had already spent the night, a bulky woman in deep mourning was hoisted in—almost like a shapeless bundle. Behind her, puffing and moaning, followed her husband—a tiny man, thin and weakly, his face death-white, his eyes small and bright and looking shy and uneasy.

The language selected by the author is filled with fresh and precise words that describe and color the two passengers as well as the setting of the excerpt. The author describes the car as "stuffy and smoky," "second-class," and "in which five people had already spent the night." All this conjures up a dreary train car. The author describes the woman as "a shapeless bundle." Her husband is "tiny," "thin," and "weakly" with a "death-white" face. These words not only lend freshness to the writing, they also clearly depict what the people look like for the reader. This is the way that a writer can color his story and the characters in it.

Role of a conclusion

The conclusion to a narrative is extremely important. It is the resolution of the story and helps the reader decide on the theme or point of the narration. The conclusion to a narrative is the resolution of the problem that is faced by the characters. A conclusion may not always be apparent; it may leave some questions unanswered. Nevertheless, a conclusion should give the reader the sense that the narrative is over, whatever the outcome. And the outcome can vary: in tragedies the conclusion is always sad, while comedies always end with a light-hearted fashion. Unlike conclusions in traditional literature, conclusions in modern literature can be much more evasive, which often leaves the reader with more questions than answers. But even this helps form the narrative and give it meaning.

Keegan is writing a story about a boy who pushes himself to become an athlete. Keegan has written about how hard the boy has trained for an upcoming race. He has noted that winning has become a huge force in his life. Now Keegan is trying to come up with a conclusion to his story. Describe what he should look for when he writes the conclusion.

Keegan should think about what the theme of the story is meant to be. Is it a story about someone who works hard and gets what he wants? Or is it about someone who loses an important race and how he deals with it? The theme should dictate the ending of the story in this case, whether he won or lost the race. A conclusion should bring the entire story to a fitting and appropriate ending so that the reader has a sense of closure. It should follow the opening and the many events that happen, so that there is a form to the story. And it should support the theme the author wants to teach.

Practice Test

Written composition

Write a composition about a time in your life when you learned an important lesson.

Sample Composition

It is a tradition in my family that we all go shopping for Thanksgiving together. Every year we buy two of everything. We buy two turkeys, two bags of potatoes, two pies, and lots of canned foods. My mom says it is important for us to go shopping as a family and really think about what we are buying. At the end of the shopping trip, we take half of the food, put it away in the house, and leave the other half in the car. Then we all get back into the car and Dad drives us to the homeless shelter. We give the shelter the rest of the food.

I did not want to go to the homeless shelter when I was younger. I wanted to stay at home and watch cartoons. I did not even want to go shopping for the food. I thought it was boring and that I had better things to do. My mom told me that I had to go and that it was very important. I remember my mom looking at the turkeys. She bought two of them. One was medium sized, and one was so big that she needed help putting it into the cart. "Go pick out some potatoes," she said to me. "And some green beans." I looked for a really long time to get the best green beans and potatoes for the shelter. It was fun to try to find the best.

When we got to the homeless shelter, people were lined up for over a block. They were all standing and wrapped in old blankets. I didn't understand. I asked my mom why they were lined up and why they were standing in the cold. She said that they did not live in a house like me and that they were lined up to get dinner for the night. She said that the shelter cooked dinner every night and gave it to the people who did not have any food or a place to live. My dad said that was why we were giving them food and why we had gone shopping. We were there so other people would have food to eat.

I now really look forward to going shopping for Thanksgiving. I try to pick the biggest turkey and the best potatoes. A few times a year my family cleans out our closets and gives old clothes, shoes, and blankets to the shelter. It still makes me sad to go to the shelter and see people standing in the cold and waiting for food, but I learned to be thankful for what I have and that it is really important to give to others.

Thank You

We at Mometrix would like to extend our heartfelt thanks to you, our friend and patron, for allowing us to play a part in your journey. It is a privilege to serve people from all walks of life who are unified in their commitment to building the best future they can for themselves.

The preparation you devote to these important testing milestones may be the most valuable educational opportunity you have for making a real difference in your life. We encourage you to put your heart into it—that feeling of succeeding, overcoming, and yes, conquering will be well worth the hours you've invested.

We want to hear your story, your struggles and your successes, and if you see any opportunities for us to improve our materials so we can help others even more effectively in the future, please share that with us as well. **The team at Mometrix would be absolutely thrilled to hear from you!** So please, send us an email (support@mometrix.com) and let's stay in touch.

If you'd like some additional help, check out these other resources we offer for your exam:

http://MometrixFlashcards.com/terranova

Additional Bonus Material

Due to our efforts to try to keep this book to a manageable length, we've created a link that will give you access to all of your additional bonus material.

Please visit http://www.mometrix.com/bonus948/terrag6 to access the information.